GETTING THE MOST
OUT OF EPHESIANS

J. Scott Duvall

Getting the Most out of Ephesians

Your Guide to Enriching Personal and Group Study

LEXHAM PRESS

Cover design: Frank Gutbrod
Interior design: { In a Word } www.inawordbooks.com

To all who have been a part of the Duvall K-Group:
Thank you for being community for Judy and me
and for helping us experience many of the realities
revealed so beautifully in Ephesians

CONTENTS

Overview of Ephesians   1

1.   Introduction to the Letter   9
     Ephesians 1:1–2

2.   Praise for Spiritual Blessings in Christ (Part 1)   16
     Ephesians 1:3–6

3.   Praise for Spiritual Blessings in Christ (Part 2)   22
     Ephesians 1:7–14

4.   Prayer for Spiritual Understanding   29
     Ephesians 1:15–23

5.   New Life in Christ (Part 1)   36
     Ephesians 2:1–7

6.   New Life in Christ (Part 2)   43
     Ephesians 2:8–10

7.   The Creation of a New Community (Part 1)   50
     Ephesians 2:11–18

8.   The Creation of a New Community (Part 2)   55
     Ephesians 2:19–22

9.   Paul's Unique Role in God's Plan   60
     Ephesians 3:1–13

10. Paul's Prayer for the New Community   67
     Ephesians 3:14–21

11. New Walk in Unity (Part 1)   73
     Ephesians 4:1–6

12. New Walk in Unity (Part 2)   79
     Ephesians 4:7–16

13. New Walk in Holiness (Part 1)   85
     Ephesians 4:17–24

14. New Walk in Holiness (Part 2)   92
     Ephesians 4:25–32

15. New Walk in Love   98
     Ephesians 5:1–6

16. New Walk in Light 105
Ephesians 5:7–14

17. New Walk in Wisdom (Part 1) 112
Ephesians 5:15–21

18. New Walk in Wisdom (Part 2) 118
Ephesians 5:21–33

19. New Walk in Wisdom (Part 3) 124
Ephesians 6:1–4

20. New Walk in Wisdom (Part 4) 131
Ephesians 6:5–9

21. New Walk in Strength 138
Ephesians 6:10–20

22. Conclusion 145
Ephesians 6:21–24

Bibliography 151

Overview of Ephesians
How Does This Book Fit into God's Redemptive Plan?

Paul didn't write Ephesians to solve a major problem or deal with any particular crisis or emergency in a local church. Instead, he wrote a majestic but general letter to give believers the overarching view of God's great plan. He often talks in sweeping terms about God's redemptive purposes, and perhaps to our surprise, we learn that the church plays a crucial role in that plan. Paul doesn't ignore what God is going to do in the future, but he does focus on what God has already done and is doing right now—in Christ and in his church. God's plan is mentioned most directly in two passages in Ephesians:

> 1:8b–10: "With all wisdom and understanding he made known to us the mystery of his will according to his good pleasure, which he purposed in Christ, to be put into effect when the times reach their fulfillment—to bring unity to all things in heaven and on earth under Christ."

> 3:8–11: "Although I am less than the least of all the Lord's people, this grace was given me: to preach to the Gentiles the boundless riches of Christ, and to make plain to everyone the administration of this mystery, which for ages past was kept hidden in God, who created all things. His intent was that now, through the church, the manifold wisdom of God should be made known to the rulers and authorities in the heavenly realms, according to his eternal purpose that he accomplished in Christ Jesus our Lord."

As New Testament scholar Peter O'Brien writes, "Cosmic reconciliation and unity in Christ are the central message of Paul's Letter to the Ephesians."[1] The "mystery of God's will" (his master plan) is to bring unity to all things in Christ. God wants to work in our individual lives to be sure, but he is doing something much, much bigger of which we are a part. His overarching purpose is to redeem the whole of creation and what Jesus has done lies at the very heart of that plan. In Christ, people can once again have a relationship with the living God. In Christ, enemies can be reconciled. In Christ, evil powers have been defeated and will one day be destroyed.

This is where you and I come into the picture. The church is God's greatest work of art, his masterpiece. As God's purposes in Christ are worked out now in the church, all of creation can see what God is up

---

[1] O'Brien, *Ephesians*, 58.

to. The church is the preview or trailer for the greatest movie ever made. As O'Brien says, "The church is not only the pattern but also the means God is using to show that his purposes are moving triumphantly to their climax."[2]

WHY IS EPHESIANS RIGHT FOR YOU?

Paul writes to help a network of house churches stay strong in their faith. He had spent three years teaching and caring for these Ephesian Christians and he wanted to make sure they continued to follow Jesus.

Specifically, Paul wanted believers to have a deeper understanding and experience of three important realities:

- The *new life* we have in Christ
- The *new community* we belong to as a result of our relationship with Christ
- The *new walk* we are called to by Christ

In this letter Paul focuses on Jesus Christ (*new life*). The expression "in Christ" (and parallel phrases like "in the Lord" or "in him") are found almost forty times in Ephesians. God will unite and restore all of creation under one Lord—Jesus Christ (1:10). Paul also stresses unity (*new community*) through words like "unity," "one," and "with/together with," and concepts such as church, body, temple, and bride. God has brought together in community all who are in Christ. This new community is maintained and preserved as we live a lifestyle that pleases Christ (*new walk*). This new lifestyle is characterized by love for God and love for people. The theme of love appears (per thousand words) more than twice as often in Ephesians than in any other Pauline letter.[3]

New life brings us into new community and encourages a new walk. Part of the new walk includes sharing with others the new life they can have in Christ.

new life   ⟶   new community   ⟶   new walk

As you read and study and seek to live out Ephesians, don't be surprised as you see God reshape your identity and make it more secure in Christ. You won't be so easily unsettled by your circumstances when you are more solidly grounded in Christ. Also, you will probably begin to invest more in your Christian community as you see the great value God places on community. As you understand what it means to be in Christ

---

[2] Ibid., 63.

[3] Hoehner, *Ephesians*, 104.

and to live in community, I predict you will begin to see new patterns of godliness appear in your life. Spiritual growth doesn't usually happen in a linear fashion (a neat, straight line of growth). Rather, our growth is often a messy start and stop, fail and try again kind of experience. But through it all, God will use this ancient letter to the Ephesians to help you grow more and more like Jesus Christ.

WHAT WAS IT LIKE TO LIVE IN EPHESUS?

If you lived in ancient Ephesus, you would have lived on the western coast of Asia Minor (modern-day Turkey). Ephesus was a cosmopolitan and multiethnic seaport city of about 250,000 people, ranking third behind Rome and Alexandria in terms of size and importance.

Your city featured modern roads, a business market, a civic center, expensive homes, public baths, a stadium, a gymnasium, temples to various gods and emperors, a concert hall, and much more. Two particular landmarks would have been especially impressive to visitors. First, there was a *theater* that seated almost 25,000 people. This is the place where the silversmith Demetrius led the crowd to riot in opposition to Paul and the Christian message (Acts 19:23–41).

Photo 1. *Theater in Ephesus*

Photo 2. *Statue of Artemis idol*

Second, there was the *temple of Artemis*, one of the seven wonders of the ancient world. Artemis was the mother goddess of nature and fertility who was worshiped throughout the ancient world. Her statue with its combination of symbols (e.g., bulls, lions, zodiac, breasts or eggs) shows how much the Ephesians blended religions. Her famous temple is no longer standing, except for a single column in a swamp.

Ephesus wasn't just devoted to Artemis worship. It was a city of many religions and cults, including worship of the Roman emperor (Nero during the time when Paul wrote Ephesians). The city was also a center for the *practice of magic and occult arts.* In Acts 19:18–19 we read that when the new Christians gave up magic, they burned their books worth 50,000 days' wages. These new believers needed reassurance that Jesus Christ was more powerful than the evil spirits and powers associated with goddess worship, the occult, the practice of magic, emperor worship, and about fifty other gods worshiped in Ephesus.

WHAT KIND OF MINISTRY DID PAUL HAVE IN EPHESUS?

(This section traces briefly the history of Paul's connection to the Ephesian church. Don't get bogged down here so feel free to read through this at a later time if you need to.)

First Visit, Second Journey (AD 52)

After spending almost two years serving the church in Corinth (Acts 18:11), Paul went to Ephesus, accompanied by Priscilla and Aquila. He didn't stay long on his first visit. About all we know is that he conversed with the Jews in the synagogue (Acts 18:19). Although the church in Ephesus invited him to stay longer, he declined and left for Antioch. He left Priscilla and Aquila in Ephesus.

Second Visit, Third Journey (AD 53–56)

On his third missionary journey he traveled through Galatia and Phrygia and came to Ephesus (Acts 18:23; 19:1). He encountered twelve men who only knew John's baptism of repentance and he told them about Jesus (Acts 19:1–7). Paul taught in the Jewish synagogue for three months, but when some began speaking evil of "the Way" (the Christian faith), he moved to the lecture hall of Tyrannus where he taught for two years so that "all the Jews and Greeks who lived in the province of Asia heard the word of the Lord" (Acts 19:10).

Paul's ministry had a great influence on the city of Ephesus. God used him to perform miracles, cast out demons, and teach the Word (Acts 19:11–20). But God's work brought opposition. When conversions to Christ hurt sales of Artemis cult idols, the local silversmiths stirred up a riot in the theater against Paul and the Christian message (Acts 19:23–41). Paul then left Ephesus for Macedonia (Acts 20:1).

Meeting with the Elders (AD 57)

Paul spent three months of winter (AD 56–57) in Corinth, the place where he wrote Romans (Rom. 16:23). He left for Jerusalem, hoping to arrive by Pentecost (May AD 57; cf. Acts 20:16, 22). As he traveled to Jerusalem he stopped in Miletus, a short distance from Ephesus, and called for the Ephesian elders to meet him there (Acts 20:17–18). Paul spoke to these church leaders about his previous ministry among them, of his plans to go to Jerusalem, about the likelihood that they would never see him again, and of false teachers who might try to infiltrate the church at Ephesus. He commended them to God and once again mentioned his example among them. They knelt in prayer together before saying a tearful goodbye (Acts 20:18–38).

A Letter from Prison (AD 60–62)

Shortly after Paul arrived in Jerusalem he was imprisoned for stirring up trouble (Acts 21:17–23:22). After a brief time, he was transferred to Caesarea where he spent two years in prison (Acts 23:23–26:32). Paul appealed to Caesar and traveled to Rome to stand trial (Acts 27:1–28:30). Most believe that Paul wrote the letter of Ephesians during his two-year imprisonment in Rome (AD 60–62).

Later Visits?

Most likely Paul was freed from his Roman imprisonment in AD 62 and revisited many churches, including some in Asia (2 Tim. 4:13, 20). Perhaps Paul did see the Ephesian elders again after all.

How Is Ephesians Organized?

From the outline below you can see that Ephesians 1–3 focuses on God's great plan of salvation in Christ: new life and new community. These chapters form the theological foundation for the instructions and commands that follow in Ephesians 4–6, where we learn how to live out God's plan. The first half tells us who Christ is and who we are in him; the second half tells us how to live like the people we are.

1:1–2	Introduction to the Letter
1:3–14	Praise for Spiritual Blessings in Christ
1:15–23	Prayer for Spiritual Understanding
2:1–10	*New Life* in Christ
2:11–3:21	*New Community* in Christ
2:11–22	The Creation of a New Community
3:1–13	Paul's Unique Role in God's Plan
3:14–21	Paul's Prayer for the New Community
4:1–6:20	*New Walk* in Christ
4:1–16	Walk in Unity
4:17–32	Walk in Holiness
5:1–6	Walk in Love
5:7–14	Walk in Light
5:15–6:9	Walk in Wisdom
6:10–20	Walk in Strength
6:21–24	Conclusion to the Letter

HOW TO USE THIS BOOK AND MORE

Just a bit of context. This guide was originally written as a year-long small-group study for a local church, where I served as a co-pastor. We used an integrated teaching plan that included (1) a week of personal study as people worked through the guide by themselves, (2) a Sunday morning sermon that focused on the same passage, and (3) small-group time on Sunday nights (after having a meal together), where we reviewed the text and talked through the discussion questions together. It worked really well. Our Ephesians study consisted of eleven weeks in the fall and eleven weeks in the spring, and this turned out to be just about right. So you could definitely use this book for personal Bible study, but you could also use it in a church setting for your small groups.

I've used the NIV 2011 as the primary translation, but since my background is New Testament studies and Greek, the study is informed by an underlying grasp of the Greek text of Ephesians. I will often bring in other translations and make a comment about the meaning of a word or how the sentence or paragraph fits together. In particular, I've found the NET Bible and the Holman Christian Standard Bible to also be very helpful.

On commentaries, here are the books I've found most helpful and reliable in my study of Ephesians. On the more technical end, I like the commentaries by Harold Hoehner and Peter O'Brien. The volume by Clinton Arnold was published after I had completed this study, but it looks to be a terrific resource. On the less technical, more pastoral side, I like the book by Kent Hughes. The works by Klyne Snodgrass and John Stott do a good job of striking a balance between the scholarly and the devotional. There are other good commentaries on Ephesians, but I've enjoyed these the most.

ACKNOWLEDGMENTS

I would like to thank Jim Weaver for publishing *Getting the Most Out of Ephesians*. He has the much-needed vision of strengthening the church and honoring the Lord by providing enriching resources for pastors, pastors-in-training, church leaders, and serious lay students of the Bible. I'm grateful to Jim for being a faithful friend and for making resources like this available to God's people.

May the Lord be pleased.

I

Introduction to the Letter

Ephesians 1:1-2

¹ Paul, an apostle of Christ Jesus by the will of God, To God's holy people in Ephesus, the faithful in Christ Jesus: ² Grace and peace to you from God our Father and the Lord Jesus Christ.

Ancient letters began by identifying the writer and the audience (e.g., "Paul to the Ephesians") before giving a greeting (e.g., "Greetings"). Christian writers used this same form, but they would modify the content to reflect deep truths about the faith. It isn't just "Paul to the Ephesians, greetings." Instead, it is "Paul, an apostle of Christ Jesus by the will of God," and the Ephesians are identified as "God's holy people" or "saints." The typical word "greeting" (*chairein*) is even changed to "grace" (*charis*).

Paul wasn't just adding fine-sounding theological words to his vocabulary to try to impress his readers. His relationship with Jesus had radically changed his life, including the way he spoke and wrote letters. Can you think of a specific example of how your relationship with Jesus has changed the way you use words?

Paul identifies himself as "an apostle of Christ Jesus." An *apostle* is one who has been called, authorized, and sent on a mission by another. Paul is a fully authorized representative and messenger of Jesus. In wanting to "focus only on Jesus," some contemporary Christian movements suggest that the words of the apostles (including Paul) are somehow less inspired and authoritative than the words of Jesus. They are viewed as second rate.

But Paul is "an apostle of Christ Jesus by the will of God." This means that Paul's letters carry Christ's full authority. God wanted Paul to be Christ's representative. If we take Jesus' words seriously, we must also take Paul's words just as seriously because they come from Christ.

The group of people receiving this letter is identified in two ways. First, they are *"God's holy people"* (or "saints"). We mistakenly think of "saints" as people who live especially pious lives, but even the Corinthian Christians are called "saints" (1 Cor. 1:2) and they certainly had issues. The saints are people who have been set apart by God, who belong to God, who are in relationship with God through Jesus. The word "saints" is simply another word for "Christians" in the New Testament.

Second, the recipients are *"faithful."* This word does not refer to a second group of people (i.e., to the saints *and* to those who are faithful), but merely tells us more about the one group (i.e., God's holy people, that is, those who are faithful in Christ Jesus). The "faithful" describes those who exercise faith in or believe in Jesus.

How might the two words—"saints" and "faithful"—sum up what we do and what God does?

Holy Geography

" [The Ephesian Christians] have two homes, for they reside equally 'in Christ' and 'in Ephesus.' Indeed all Christian people . . . live both in Christ and in the secular world. . . . Many of our spiritual troubles arise from our failure to remember that we are citizens of two kingdoms. We tend to either pursue Christ and withdraw from the world, or to become preoccupied with the world and forget that we are also in Christ.[4] "

---

[4] Stott, *Ephesians*, 23.

Photo 3. *Street connecting the harbor and theater in Ephesus*

The original recipients of this letter were both *"in Ephesus"* and *"in Christ."* In fact, all Christians are both "in _____" (some city) and "in Christ." Paul's sense of geography or location places us both in Christ relationally and spiritually and in the world for ministry and mission. Life goes so much better when we know who we are "in Christ" and what our relationships and roles are where we live.

What exactly does it mean to be "in Christ"? Paul uses the phrase "in Christ" (and equivalents) many times in Ephesians. To be "in Christ" is to be personally related to Jesus Christ, to be united to Christ, to be one with him and his people.

To be "in Christ" means that Jesus determines our identity, our priorities, and our destiny. If you are unsure of who you are or where you are going, you might want to spend some time reflecting on the "in Christ" words below.

Paul's greeting consists of "grace and peace from God our Father and the Lord Jesus Christ." The typical word for greeting (*chairein*) is even changed to "grace" (*charis*). *Grace* is the gospel in one word. While we were undeserving sinners totally unable to save ourselves, Christ came to our rescue. Grace refers to God's favor in providing salvation through Christ for people who didn't deserve it.

Peace is deep contentment, calmness, and wholeness that comes from a harmonious relationship with God. By greeting the Ephesians (and us) in this way, Paul is reminding us that God's grace is what produces our peace. When we experience God's undeserved forgiveness and mercy, we are flooded with a sense of well-being.

IN CHRIST

Often the phrase "in Christ" refers to the relational place where believers are positioned. Just as all people have died "in Adam" (1 Cor. 15:22) and all the

In many Bibles you will see a text note on verse 1 that says something like "some early manuscripts do not include the words 'in Ephesus.'" It is possible that this letter was intended not only for the Ephesian church, but also for other churches in the region (i.e., a circular letter). Harold Hoehner makes a good case, however, for the phrase "in Ephesus" being part of the original text (Hoehner, *Ephesians*, 144–48). Whether it was in the original letter or not, the letter became connected with the Ephesian church at an early stage because Ephesus was the dominant city in the region.

nations will be blessed "in Abraham" (Gen. 12:3; 18:18), so all Christians have been incorporated into Christ. As believers, our relationship with Christ is *the* defining relationship. This relationship is the reality center that shapes all our activities and relationships. At other times, the phrase "in Christ" means that Christ is the agent or instrument through whom something is done. For example, in 1:4 the church ("us" not "me") was chosen "in Christ" before the foundation of the world. This means that God chose the church through Christ's work of paying for sin on the cross.

1:1	"To God's holy people in Ephesus, the faithful *in Christ Jesus*"
1:3	"who has blessed us in the heavenly realms with every spiritual blessing *in Christ*"
1:4	"For he chose us *in him* before the creation of the world to be holy and blameless in his sight."
1:6	"to the praise of his glorious grace, which he has freely given us *in the One he loves*"
1:7	"*In him* we have redemption through his blood, the forgiveness of sins."
1:9	"He made known to us the mystery of his will according to his good pleasure, which he purposed *in Christ*."
1:10	"to bring unity to all things in heaven and on earth *under Christ*"
1:11	"*In him* we were also chosen."
1:12	"in order that we, who were the first to put our hope *in Christ*, might be for the praise of his glory"
1:13	"And you also were included *in Christ* when you heard the message of truth, the gospel of your salvation. When you believed, you were marked *in him* with a seal, the promised Holy Spirit."
1:15	"ever since I heard about your faith *in the Lord Jesus* and your love for all God's people"
1:20	"he exerted [*in Christ*] when he raised Christ from the dead"
2:5	"made us alive *with Christ* even when we were dead in transgressions"
2:6	"And God raised us up *with Christ* and seated us *with him* in the heavenly realms in Christ Jesus."
2:7	"the incomparable riches of his grace, expressed in his kindness to us *in Christ Jesus*"

2:10	"For we are God's handiwork, created *in Christ Jesus* to do good works."
2:13	"But now *in Christ Jesus* you who once were far away have been brought near."
2:15	"His purpose was to create *in himself* one new humanity out of the two."
2:16	"to reconcile both of them to God through the cross, by which he put to death their hostility [*in him*]"
2:21	"*In him* the whole building is joined together and rises to become a holy temple *in the Lord*."
2:22	"And *in him* you too are being built together to become a dwelling in which God lives by his Spirit."
3:6	"sharers together in the promise *in Christ Jesus*"
3:11	"according to his eternal purpose that he accomplished *in Christ Jesus our Lord*"
3:12	"*In him* and through faith *in him* we may approach God with freedom and confidence."
3:21	"to him be glory in the church and *in Christ Jesus* throughout all generations"
4:1	"As a prisoner *for [in] the Lord*, then, I urge you to live a life worthy of the calling."
4:15	"We will grow to become in every respect the mature body *of [into] him* who is the head, that is, Christ."
4:17	"So I tell you this, and insist on it *in the Lord*, that you must no longer live as the Gentiles do."
4:21	"when you heard about Christ and were taught *in him* in accordance with the truth that is *in Jesus*"
4:32	"Be kind and compassionate to one another, forgiving each other, just as *in Christ* God forgave you."
5:8	"For you were once darkness, but now you are light *in the Lord*."
5:20	"giving thanks to God the Father for everything, *in the name of our Lord Jesus Christ*"
6:1	"Children, obey your parents *in the Lord*, for this is right."
6:10	"Finally, be strong *in the Lord* and in his mighty power."
6:21	"Tychicus, the dear brother and faithful servant *in the Lord*, will tell you everything."

SO WHAT?

1. What struggles or opportunities do you think we have in common with the Christians who lived in ancient Ephesus?

2. As you begin your study of Ephesians, what excites you most about exploring this amazing letter?

3. What happens when the way we speak and live is not affected by our faith? Does this mean that we are being sensitive to our culture by avoiding unnecessary religious lingo, or does it say that our faith doesn't really have much of an influence over the way we live? Or some of both?

4. How would you evaluate your own "geography" (i.e., "in Ephesus" and "in Christ")? How would you like that to change?

5. The expression "in Christ" is one of the most important phrases in the entire New Testament. This little phrase speaks about our oneness, identity, and relationship with Jesus. How would you explain to a friend in plain language what it means to be "in Christ"?

2

Praise for Spiritual Blessings in Christ (Part I)

Ephesians 1:3-6

[3] Praise be to the God and Father of our Lord Jesus Christ, who has blessed us in the heavenly realms with every spiritual blessing in Christ. [4] For he chose us in him before the creation of the world to be holy and blameless in his sight. In love [5] he predestined us for adoption to sonship through Jesus Christ, in accordance with his pleasure and will—[6] to the praise of his glorious grace, which he has freely given us in the One he loves.

> Psalm 72:18–19:
> "*Blessed* be the Lord, the God of Israel, who alone does wondrous things. *Blessed* be his glorious name forever; may the whole earth be filled with his glory! Amen and Amen!"

Most of Paul's letters begin with a thanksgiving and a prayer, but Ephesians explodes in praise: "*Praise* be (or blessed be) to the God . . . who has *blessed* us . . . with every spiritual *blessing*." The form Paul uses here appears in many Old Testament Psalms. Sometimes God is praised for who he is, but most often in Scripture God is praised because of what he has done for us. God blesses us and we in turn praise God. Worship is our response to God's character and to his blessings. When your worship of God has been the deepest and richest, has there also been a special awareness of what God has done for you? If so, what brought these blessings to your attention?

Notice how Paul praises the Triune God (Father, Son, and Spirit) in 1:3–14 for all he has done for believers. In your own words describe the blessings that Paul mentions in this passage:

Each section ends with a similar phrase: "to the praise of his glorious grace" (1:6, 12, 14), showing that God's blessings cause us to recognize his glory and praise him even more.

In 1:4–6 Paul mentions the Father's blessing of choosing, or electing, us as his people. Election is certainly a biblical doctrine, but one that is often misunderstood and misapplied. In addition, many people go beyond what the Bible actually says in an attempt to build a theological system that somehow improves upon Scripture. Much damage has come to the cause of Christ by those who refuse to acknowledge the biblical tension between God's sovereignty and human freedom. My hope and prayer for you is that you will lay aside secondary sources and focus again on what God is saying through the primary source of his Word. After all, we are not disciples of John Calvin, Jonathan Edwards, or Jacob Arminius; we are first and foremost followers of Jesus Christ.

What does this passage teach about election? First, you will notice that the pronouns referring to believers are plural. God has chosen "us" (not "me") that "we" (not "I") should be holy and blameless. God has predestined "us" (not "me") to adoption as his children. Nothing in Ephesians 1 focuses on the individual. Election is primarily a *corporate concept*. Paul is not saying that God chose one individual for heaven and another for hell before they were even born. Rather, he is saying that God's eternal plan included having a people to call his own. In his sovereignty God determined that he would save a people. There is nothing that could keep God from having a people.

In the Old Testament God chose Abraham as the head of a people, Israel (Gen. 12:1–3). God chose Israel to be his holy people so that all the nations on earth would be blessed through them (Deut. 7:6; 10:15; 14:2). In the New Testament God chose Jesus Christ to be the head of his people, the church. The apostle Peter applies terms once applied to Israel to the church. The church is God's chosen people:

> But you are a chosen people, a royal priesthood, a holy nation, God's special possession, that you may declare the praises of him who called you out of darkness into his wonderful light. Once you were not a people, but now you are the people of God; once you had not received mercy, but now you have received mercy. (1 Pet. 2:9–10)

Heavenly Realms?

This strange phrase is not another expression for "heaven." Literally the phrase reads "in the heavenlies" and is used in Ephesians in 1:20 and 2:6, where Christ and believers are exalted; in 3:10, where God reveals his wisdom to rulers and authorities; and in 6:12, where believers battle evil forces. The phrase "heavenly realms" does not refer to a physical location, but to "the unseen world of spiritual reality" (Stott, *Ephesians*, 35). While Christians enjoy physical life in a physical world created by God, there is a larger unseen reality where Christ has already been exalted as Lord, where we experience God's blessings, and where we still battle evil forces.

Second, election is *"in Christ."* We have been chosen "in him" (1:4) and predestined for adoption "through Jesus" (1:5) and these blessings are bestowed upon us "in the One he loves" (1:6). In the Old Testament, God chose Israel to be his people. In the New Testament era, God has chosen the church (followers of Jesus the Messiah) to be his people. Christ is the "seed of Abraham" (Gal. 3) who fulfills Israel's election. Before the foundation of the world, God determined that those "in Christ" would be his people.

The order is important: "Individuals are not elected and then put in Christ. They are in Christ [by grace through faith] and therefore elect."[5] God graciously invites all to become part of this people (1 Tim. 2:3–4), but only those who respond to his grace by faith in Christ will join his community. Throughout Ephesians 1, faith in Christ is clearly emphasized as essential to a relationship with God—1:1, 13, 15, 19. As William Klein says, "Election is not a prior selection by God that excludes non-chosen individuals from salvation. God has chosen a people in Christ, but individuals must decide whether or not to accept God's salvation and so enter that body (Rom. 10:13)."[6]

Third, the purpose of election is *transformational.* God determined that his people would be "holy and blameless in his sight" and that they would be his precious children by adoption through Jesus. Election brings privilege (adoption), but also responsibility (holy and blameless).

> **Colossians 1:21–23:**
> "Once you were alienated from God and were enemies in your minds because of your evil behavior. But now he has reconciled you by Christ's physical body through death to present you holy in his sight, without blemish and free from accusation—if you continue in your faith, established and firm, and do not move from the hope held out in the gospel. This is the gospel that you heard and that has been proclaimed to every creature under heaven, and of which I, Paul, have become a servant."

The words "holy and blameless" were used in the Old Testament to describe unblemished animals presented to God as sacrifices (Exod. 29:37–38; cf. Heb. 9:14; 1 Pet. 1:19). Here in Ephesians 1, these words remind us that God chose us so that we might become like Jesus (Rom. 8:29). In Colossians, Paul uses these same words to say something similar. We will not become completely holy and blameless until we appear "before him" at his second coming. Until then, God continues the project of transforming us into the image of Jesus.

There are better reasons for taking "in love" with "holy and blameless" than with "predestined" (see, e.g., ESV, NET).[7] God's goal is that his people should be not only pure and holy, but also loving toward one another. When holiness forsakes love (read Jesus' words to the Ephesian church in

---

5 Snodgrass, *Ephesians*, 49.

6 Klein, *Chosen People*, 267.

7 O'Brien, *Ephesians*, 101–102.

Rev. 2:1–7), then it ceases to be true holiness. God calls us to holy love and loving holiness—both flow out of the character of God.

God's chosen people have been adopted as his children through the work of Christ. Under Roman law adoption was an incredible privilege that brought all the rights of a natural child. A privilege once belonging to Israel (Rom. 9:4) now belongs to the church (Rom. 9:26; 2 Cor. 6:18). How does it make you feel that God has adopted you? (We all need to belong so get beyond a surface answer here.)

The refrain "to the praise of his glorious grace" marks the end of this section (see also 1:12, 14). When we think about the Father's plan to save a people, we praise him for his grace. The attention now turns to Jesus (the Beloved). We are invited to join the chosen community through all that Christ has done for us.

We Belong

" We all desire relationships in which we are accepted, valued, and wanted. We desperately long for this esteem from our peers, but seldom experience the 'real thing.' Countless stories are written about teenagers who accept life-threatening dares in the hopes of being accepted by their peers, or business people who compromise their integrity and ethics to join an elite, inner circle. We read of men and women who are driven to succeed because they believe the lie that says their value is determined by the quality and level of their performance. Or how about the teenager or lonely single who sacrifices his virginity for the chance to experience closeness and the feeling of being wanted? For the Christian, none of this futile struggle is necessary because we have been chosen by God before time ever began. We belong, we matter, we have been accepted. No longer outcasts or second-class citizens, we are part of his family.[8] **"**

So What?

1. Do you ever struggle with a lack of desire to worship God? If so, do you think this might be connected to a lack of awareness of all that God has done for you? How could that change?

2. Which of the blessings that Paul mentions in 1:3–14 means the most to you at this point in your life? Why?

---

[8] Smalley and Trent, *Dad's Blessing*, 26.

3. What comes to your mind when someone mentions the "doctrine of election"?

4. We observed in Ephesians 1 that election is corporate, connected with Christ, and transformational. How does this emphasis in the text change your previous understanding of election?

5. How does your church bring praise to God's glory? How could we bring even more?

3

PRAISE FOR SPIRITUAL BLESSINGS IN CHRIST (PART 2)

Ephesians 1:7-14

7 In him we have redemption through his blood, the forgiveness of sins, in accordance with the riches of God's grace 8 that he lavished on us. With all wisdom and understanding, 9 he made known to us the mystery of his will according to his good pleasure, which he purposed in Christ, 10 to be put into effect when the times reach their fulfillment—to bring unity to all things in heaven and on earth under Christ. 11 In him we were also chosen, having been predestined according to the plan of him who works out everything in conformity with the purpose of his will, 12 in order that we, who were the first to put our hope in Christ, might be for the praise of his glory. 13 And you also were included in Christ when you heard the message of truth, the gospel of your salvation. When you believed, you were marked in him with a seal, the promised Holy Spirit, 14 who is a deposit guaranteeing our inheritance until the redemption of those who are God's possession—to the praise of his glory.

Before the foundation of the world, the Father came up with a plan to rescue people from sin and Satan. The Son carried out the plan through his life, death, and resurrection. The Holy Spirit now makes the plan a personal reality to those who respond to God's gracious offer. God must really love us!

Some of the blessings that come from the Son include redemption and forgiveness, overflowing grace, spiritual wisdom to understand God's master plan, and our belonging to God as his inheritance. Again, all this results in God's praise and God's glory.

The word "redemption" in verse 7 involves release from bondage through the payment of a price or ransom. In this case the price is the "blood" of Christ—the sacrifice of his life on the cross on our behalf. The result of redemption is the "forgiveness of sins." Setting us free from slavery to sin was costly. Jesus paid the ransom with his life. This explains why

Photo 4. *Christian symbols at Ephesus*

he is often called the "Lamb of God." Consider the following passages that focus on Christ's redemptive work:

1 Peter 1:18–19—"For you know that it was not with perishable things such as silver or gold that you were redeemed from the empty way of life handed down to you from your ancestors, but with the precious blood of Christ, a lamb without blemish or defect."

Hebrews 9:12—"He did not enter by means of the blood of goats and calves; but he entered the Most Holy Place once for all by his own blood, thus obtaining eternal redemption."

Mark 10:45—"For even the Son of Man did not come to be served, but to serve, and to give his life as a ransom for many."

Revelation 5:9–12—"And they sang a new song, saying: 'You are worthy to take the scroll and to open its seals, because you were slain, and with your blood you purchased for God persons from every tribe and language and people and nation. You have made them to be a kingdom and priests to serve our God, and they will reign on the earth.' . . . 'Worthy is the Lamb, who was slain, to receive power and wealth and wisdom and strength and honor and glory and praise!'"

In Christ we have been forgiven. Totally forgiven! Can you recall a time in your life when you felt God's guilt-destroying, burden-lifting, conscious-cleansing forgiveness? Write a short description of that experience.

Redemption and forgiveness in Christ are "in accordance with the riches of God's grace." What is the difference between God giving "in accordance with his grace" and God giving "out of his grace"? Think of it this way, would you rather a rich person give you a gift "out of their riches" or "according to their riches"? Why?

Slave Trader to Slave of Christ

Check out the story of John Newton, a wretched slave trader who experienced God's forgiveness in spite of his sinful past. He later wrote the hymn *Amazing Grace*. http://www.christianitytoday .com/ch/131christians/ pastorsandpreachers/newton.html

God's grace also brings "wisdom and understanding" as he shows us what he is up to in Christ. He has given us spiritual discernment or understanding so that we will know "the mystery of his will."

The word "mystery" refers to something previously hidden that has now been revealed (see Eph. 1:9; 3:3, 4, 9; 5:32; 6:19). It's like a secret, but an open secret for God's people. The mystery cannot be discovered by human wisdom alone. Rather, God has shown his people his master plan to "bring unity to all things in heaven and on earth under Christ."

Christ is the one in whom God sums up the cosmos. This Greek word translated "bring unity" was used to describe adding up a column of numbers, of bringing a speech to a conclusion, or of gathering troops under one commander. The entire universe was fragmented and scattered by sin. But one day God will restore his universe to unity under one supreme king—Jesus. As my old Greek teacher Curtis Vaughan put it, "The ultimate destiny of the universe now rests in the hands that once were nailed to the cross."[9]

In Christ we were also "chosen" or "received an inheritance" (HCSB). Most of the leading commentators say that this phrase is better understood to mean that we have become God's inheritance. In the Old Testament, Israel was God's personal possession, as Deuteronomy 32:8–9 says: "But the LORD's portion is his people, Jacob his own inheritance" (see also Deut. 4:20; 9:29; Ps. 33:12; 106:40). If you have been wondering what God gets out of sending his precious Son to pay the price for our sins, the answer is—us! We are God's inheritance. We are what God gets out of the deal. Long ago God decided that he wanted a people, a community (see the rest of v. 11).

According to 1:12, what is our purpose as God's special, chosen people?

Photo 5. *Statue of a woman representing virtue of wisdom (SOFIA) at Library of Celsus in Ephesus*

In 1:13–14, we come to the blessings of the Holy Spirit:

Heard the gospel ⟶ Believed in Jesus Christ ⟶ Sealed with the Spirit

---

[9] Vaughan, *Ephesians*, 26.

When people hear the word of truth (the gospel) and believe in Jesus, they are sealed with the Holy Spirit. The word "seal" is a powerful word that indicates ownership. Animals (and even slaves in the ancient world) were branded with a seal. When we trust Christ, God stamps us with a seal—the Holy Spirit. The Holy Spirit indicates that we truly belong to God (2 Cor. 1:22; Rom. 8:9).

The Holy Spirit is the "deposit guaranteeing" our inheritance. This expression refers to a down payment or first installment of full payment to be made at a later date. Our redemption in Christ is real, but it is not complete. We still sin. We still fight spiritual battles. We still suffer and die. There will come a day when God will destroy Satan, kill death, give us resurrected bodies, and live with us in a new heaven and a new earth. We long for that time. This world is not our home. How do we know this is really going to happen? How do we know that God is going to keep his promise? Answer: the Holy Spirit! The Spirit is God's way of saying, "Here is a taste of my Presence. Here is my guarantee that I have a perfect future in store for you. You are secure and safe and I will protect you until that day. What I started in your life, I will finish and nothing can separate you from my love."

Look back at all of 1:3–14 and rewrite this explosion of praise in your own words:

So What?

1. What are some of the powers that enslave people today (e.g., fear, lust, addiction to social media, lies)? Since those enemies truly enslave and destroy people, how can those of us who have been redeemed and forgiven in Christ resist returning to these same old horrible masters?

2. God lavishes his grace on us. Describe your most vivid experience of the super abundant grace of God.

3. If God has made known to his people the "mystery of his will" to "bring unity to all things" in Christ, why do God's people sometimes seem so ignorant of his will? What can we do about it?

4. As God's inheritance, we are extremely valuable. But we exist "for the praise of his glory," not our own (1:12, 14). How can we keep from letting our "importance" overwhelm or undermine our purpose to glorify God?

5. What do the promised blessings from the Holy Spirit mean to you (seal, down payment)?

4

PRAYER FOR SPIRITUAL UNDERSTANDING

Ephesians 1:15-23

15 For this reason, ever since I heard about your faith in the Lord Jesus and your love for all God's people, 16 I have not stopped giving thanks for you, remembering you in my prayers. 17 I keep asking that the God of our Lord Jesus Christ, the glorious Father, may give you the Spirit of wisdom and revelation, so that you may know him better. 18 I pray that the eyes of your heart may be enlightened in order that you may know the hope to which he has called you, the riches of his glorious inheritance in his holy people, 19 and his incomparably great power for us who believe. That power is the same as the mighty strength 20 he exerted when he raised Christ from the dead and seated him at his right hand in the heavenly realms, 21 far above all rule and authority, power and dominion, and every name that is invoked, not only in the present age but also in the one to come. 22 And God placed all things under his feet and appointed him to be head over everything for the church, 23 which is his body, the fullness of him who fills everything in every way.

Do you ever have trouble grasping what God has done for you? In our last study (1:3–14), we learned that God has blessed us with every spiritual blessing in Christ. Yet because we live in an instant society, a "McWorld," with very little memory of what happened five minutes ago, we often find it hard to take in and remember what God has done for us. We're moving too fast. Perhaps that's the reason why the very next section of Ephesians is a prayer asking for God's help. After describing God's blessings in 1:3–14, Paul offers a prayer in 1:15–23 asking for spiritual wisdom to comprehend those blessings. Without God's help, we just won't get it. May Paul's prayer become our prayer.

Here is how 1:15–23 is organized:

1:15–16	The reason for the prayer
1:17–18a	The request itself—that God may give you the Spirit of wisdom and revelation
1:18b	The basis of the prayer—the eyes of your heart have been enlightened
1:18c	The purpose of the prayer—in order that you may know
1:18d–19	The content of the prayer
1:18d	The hope to which God has called us
1:18e	The riches of God's glorious inheritance in us
1:19	The greatness of God's power for us
1:20–23	The evidence of God's power at work in Christ:
1:20a	Raised Christ from the dead
1:20b–21	Seated Christ at God's right hand
1:22a	Put all things under Christ's feet
1:22b–23	Appointed Christ to be head over everything for the church

The phrase "for this reason" in verse 15 probably points back to the whole preceding section—1:3–14. Because of all that God has done for these believers and because of their faith in Christ and love for each other, Paul prays for them. Underline or highlight the different words for prayer used in 1:16–17. What do you think these words say to us about prayer?

The heart of this prayer is that God the Father "may give you the Spirit of wisdom and revelation, so that you may know him better" (1:17). Paul is not asking that these people be given the Holy Spirit for the first time, since they had already received the Spirit (see 1:13–14), or that they be given a so-called second blessing from the Spirit. Rather, this is a prayer for a greater understanding of God's plan in Christ and for the wisdom to live in light of that plan. Here Paul is praying that the Spirit would help us grasp what God has done for us.

Photo 6. *St. John's Basilica in Ephesus, perhaps the place where John is buried*

This prayer is based on the fact that "the eyes of your heart have been enlightened" (1:18 NET). If the "heart" refers to the center of a person's being (mind, emotions, will), what do you think Paul means by "the eyes of your heart"?

If God answered our prayers for "a Spirit of wisdom and revelation, so that you may know him better," what would that look like in someone's life? The answer relates to three specific things that Paul asks for next. The Spirit helps us connect to God's plan by helping us grasp these three realities. Explain in your own words what you think each one means.

"The hope to which God has called us"

"The riches of God's glorious inheritance in us"

"God's incomparably great power for us"

We pray that the Holy Spirit will help us to comprehend the future God has for us, how much God loves and values us, and the power God has given us. In 1:19 alone there are four different words for power that show God's great and amazing work in our lives—"power" (*dunamis*), "exercise" or working (*energeia*), "immense" or mighty (*kratos*), and "strength" (*ischus*).

Although Paul piles up the words for power in verse 19, it's almost as if he can't find enough words to say what he wants to say. As a result, he turns to the supreme illustration of God's power in Jesus. God displayed his power by accomplishing four things for Christ:

- *Raised Jesus from the dead* (1:20a)—Jesus really died. Throughout Scripture we are told that God raised him from the dead, not just from a state of death, but "out from the dead ones" (we too will be raised from the dead one day). His resurrection is the greatest demonstration of God's power (Rom. 1:4; 1 Cor. 6:14; Phil. 3:10).
- *Seated (exalted) Jesus at God's right hand* (1:20b–21)—Jesus' exaltation is different from his resurrection. As Murray Harris says, "The Resurrection proclaims 'He lives' [and] the Exaltation proclaims 'He reigns.'"[10] With his God-given mission accomplished, Jesus was given a special place of honor and authority "at God's right hand," meaning that Jesus now shares God's throne—the center of all reality (Ps. 110:1).
- *Put all things under Jesus' feet* (1:22a)—Whatever powers exist (human or non-human), they are all subject to Christ: rule, authority, power, dominion, and name, now and forever. Every conceivable power has been placed under the authority and reign of Jesus Christ (Ps. 8:6).
- *Gave Jesus as head over all things to the church* (1:22b–23)—Christ is head over all things for the benefit of the church, his body. Although 1:23 is very difficult to understand, it basically means that in Christ God has revealed his presence and power, that Christ is head over the church, and that the church as Christ's body may rely on and draw from Christ's fullness (see 4:15–16 for a similar idea).

Connected to the Power Source?

❝ Just before World War II in the town of Itasca, Texas, a school fire took the lives of 263 children. There was scarcely a family in the town which was not touched by this horrifying tragedy. During the war Itasca remained without school facilities. But when the war ended, the town, like many others, began to expand and in fact built a new school, which featured what was called "the finest sprinkler system in the world." Civic pride ran high. Honor students were selected to guide citizens and visitors on tours of the new facility to show them the finest, most advanced sprinkler system technology could supply and money could buy. Never again

---

[10] Harris, *Raised Immortal*, 85.

would Itasca be visited by such a tragedy. With the postwar boom the town continued to grow, and seven years later it was necessary to enlarge the school—and in adding the new wing it was discovered that the sprinkler system had never been connected. Can you believe it? How unthinkable that the sprinkler system was never connected. Yet the story is also a parable of what happens with many Christians. God has given us the power we need to glorify him and transform this world, but many of us never 'connect' and our lives remain impotent and useless. Are you trying to live as a Christian in your own 'strength'?"[11] "

So What?

1. If you prayed 1:15–23 for a friend (and praying Scripture is a great thing), what changes would you expect to see in your friend as God began to answer your prayer?

2. At this point in your life, what part of this prayer do you need someone to pray for you?

[11] Hughes, *Ephesians*, 57.

3. What prevents us from connecting to the power that God has already made available to us?

4. Coming out of a background of magic, the Artemis cult or astrological beliefs, many of the Ephesian Christians lived in great fear of hostile spiritual powers. How would Paul's words comfort them? How do Paul's words offer you personal encouragement?

5. God's power raised Jesus from the dead, exalted him to the highest authority, made all powers subject to him, and gave him as head over all things to the church—this power is the same power that is available to us. What are some practical, specific ways we can connect to God's awesome power?

5

NEW LIFE IN CHRIST (PART 1)

Ephesians 2:1–7

¹ As for you, you were dead in your transgressions and sins, ² in which you used to live when you followed the ways of this world and of the ruler of the kingdom of the air, the spirit who is now at work in those who are disobedient. ³ All of us also lived among them at one time, gratifying the cravings of our flesh and following its desires and thoughts. Like the rest, we were by nature deserving of wrath. ⁴ But because of his great love for us, God, who is rich in mercy, ⁵ made us alive with Christ even when we were dead in transgressions—it is by grace you have been saved. ⁶ And God raised us up with Christ and seated us with him in the heavenly realms in Christ Jesus, ⁷ in order that in the coming ages he might show the incomparable riches of his grace, expressed in his kindness to us in Christ Jesus.

After Paul introduces the letter (1:1–2), praises God for all his blessings (1:3–14), and prays that we would grasp all that God has done (1:15–23), he turns his attention to our new life in Christ (2:1–10). But this section begins with death rather than life.

Verses 1–7 actually form one long sentence in Greek, organized in the following way:

Subject:	"God" (v. 4)
Main verbs:	"made alive with" (v. 5),
	"raised up with" (v. 6),
	"seated with" (v. 6)
Object:	"us"

Why does Paul wait until verse 4 before getting to the main part of the sentence? Because he wants us to remember how totally and absolutely dead we were before we found life in Jesus. In 2:1–3 Paul offers a lengthy description of our spiritual condition before coming to Christ ("you were dead . . ."). He wants us to feel the weight of our spiritual problem before we experience the solution in verse 4. We were dead in our sins—not sick, not struggling, not even dying . . . dead!

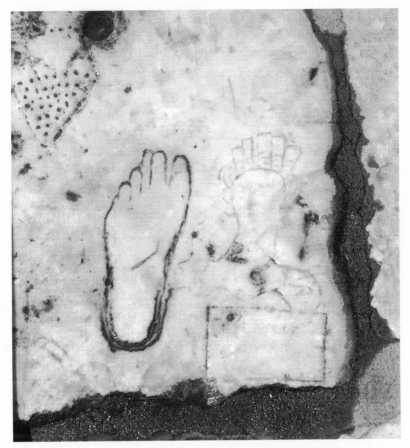

Photo 7. *Directions to a brothel carved in the Marble Street in Ephesus. The heart, foot, and woman show the way to the house of "love," perhaps for those who could not read.*

The two words "transgressions and sins" form one idea. Without Christ, people are alienated and separated from God. According to Paul, people live in one of two spheres or domains of influence—either in sin(s) or in Christ.

The term for "live" (or "walk") refers to the overall direction and conduct of a person's life. People who live in "transgressions and sins" are spiritually dead since there is nothing they can do to help themselves. Within the sphere of sin, people are enslaved by three specific evil forces. After reading the brief definition of each, answer the questions that follow.

The world: the attitudes, ideas, habits, and commitments of people who reject God (2:2a).

The devil: a reference to Satan, the ruler of the powers of darkness (2:2b).

The flesh: our self-centered tendency to go our own way and ignore God (2:3a).

How do you see these three powers working together today to enslave people without Christ? How do Christians sometimes subject themselves all over again to these three forces?

The bottom line is that apart from a relationship with Jesus Christ we are "deserving of wrath." The wrath Paul mentions in verse 3 is God's holy anger against sin that results in his judgment. Apart from Christ, we deserve (and are destined for) God's punishment.

From Death to Life

❝ Some years ago as a youth pastor I hiked with some of my high schoolers to the top of Mt. Whitney in California, the highest spot in the continental United States (14,495 feet). We exulted over the wonderful panorama of the Sierra Nevadas and the Mojave Desert.... As we gazed together from what seemed to be the top of the world, one of our party pointed out that only eighty miles to the southeast was Death Valley, the lowest spot in the United States at 280 feet below sea level and the hottest place in the country with a record 134 degrees in the shade! What a contrast! One place is the top of the world, the other the bottom. One place is perpetually cool, the other relentlessly hot. From Mt. Whitney you look down on all of life. From Death Valley you can only look up to the rest of the world. In Ephesians 2 Paul takes us down to the Death Valley of the soul (vv. 1-3) and then to 'the heavenly realms in Christ Jesus' (vv. 4-7).[12] 〞

Paul uses the literary device of contrast to move from the place of death to the place of life. In your own words identify all the contrasts you can find in 2:1-7, either stated or implied:

The two greatest words in the Bible are "But . . . God" (v. 4). We were spiritually dead—walking in the ways of the world, enslaved by Satan, doing whatever we felt like doing, destined for God's condemnation . . . hopeless and helpless. BUT GOD!

Why didn't God leave us in our spiritual graves? What motivated him to come to our rescue? What are the four words that describe God's compassionate character? (It's really good to remember that God's actions flow out of his character or his heart.)

- _____ (v. 4)

- _____ (v. 4)

- _____ (vv. 5, 7, 8)

- _____ (v. 7)

What did God actually do for us? Notice the three main verbs in 2:5-6: made us alive, raised us up, and seated us, and all of this happened in connection "with Christ." Mysteriously we share in Christ's resurrection (made alive), ascension (raised up), and exaltation (seated). What

---

[12] Hughes, *Ephesians*, 65.

happened to Jesus also happened to us (see 1:20). But how? We are living two thousand years after the time of Christ. How could we be connected to Christ's resurrection and exaltation? Any ideas?

By Grace You Are Saved
The form of the verb "saved" refers to a past event (accomplished by Christ) with present and ongoing results—we have been saved and continue in a state of being saved from death, slavery, and wrath.

Perhaps we find some help in understanding how this happens when we stop thinking only about the individual and start thinking more about the community. Jesus wasn't just an individual, but also a new Adam heading up a whole new race of people (see Rom. 5; 1 Cor. 15). As people in relationship with Christ, we are part of this new community (remember 1:22–23 where Christ is the head of the church, which is his body?). As Robert Tannehill says, "Christ's death and resurrection are not merely events which produce benefits for the believer but are events in which the believer participates."[13] Although we weren't literally there when Jesus was resurrected, in some mysterious but real way, we were there. We were buried with Christ. We were made alive with Christ. We were raised up and exalted with Christ. We don't just get gifts from him, we are put into a relationship with him and participate in his life.

God's purpose in saving us is to "show the incomparable riches of his grace, expressed in his kindness to us in Christ Jesus" (v. 7). In other words, we are trophies of God's grace. Remember the expression in 1:6, 12, 14—"to the praise of his glory"? When God rescues flawed, sinful,

---

[13] Tannehill, *Dying and Rising*, 1.

rebellious, confused, faithless, messed up, spiritually dead people like us, the universe marvels at the mercy, love, grace, and kindness of God. We always come back to worship.

SO WHAT?

1. Of the three basic views of human nature (humans are healthy, humans are sick, humans are dead), which one does this passage support? Which one is most popular in our culture? What are the results or consequences associated with each view?

2. Why do you think Paul would remind these Christians of their pre-Christian spiritual condition?

3. What do you remember about the time in your life when you were spiritually dead? Some of us came to Christ at an early age and we don't have vivid memories of what it was like to be spiritually dead.

How can we become more aware of what it means to be separated from God?

4. What do the words "But God" in verse 4 mean to you?

5. As you read about God's character (the four words) and God's actions toward us (three main verbs), what means the most to you at this point in your life?

6. If we have been made alive, raised up, and seated with Christ (alive on Mt. Whitney), why do we sometimes prefer to walk around in Death Valley?

6

NEW LIFE IN CHRIST (PART 2)

Ephesians 2:8-10

⁸ For it is by grace you have been saved, through faith—and this is not from yourselves, it is the gift of God—⁹ not by works, so that no one can boast. ¹⁰ For we are God's handiwork, created in Christ Jesus to do good works, which God prepared in advance for us to do.

In 2:8–10 we have the gospel in a nutshell. Here we see in a few sentences what it really means to be a Christian. There is no better summary of the Christian message anywhere in the Bible. This is indeed a view from the mountaintop.

The phrase "you have been saved" emphasizes the accomplishment and ongoing results of our salvation. We have been saved and continue in a state of being saved. In other words, we are safe and secure in God's hands.

The foundation or basis of this salvation is God's grace. Christians are saved "by grace." Grace is God's love for, acceptance of, and goodness toward those who don't deserve it and are unable to achieve it—all of us.

We are not saved "by faith" but "through faith." Faith is not a human work that earns God's salvation, but rather a means by which we receive salvation. When we have "faith" as the Bible defines it, we believe certain things about God (our head), we trust and have confidence in God as one who is true and trustworthy (our hearts), and we respond to God through our actions (our hands). So grace is the basis and faith is the means of salvation. Grace is what makes salvation possible and faith is how we receive it—"by grace through faith." To confuse the basis and the means can spell spiritual disaster for us.

In your own words, explain or illustrate what you have just read about the relationship between grace and faith. You might think about how you would explain it to someone else.

Accepting the Gift

> The salvation that was purchased by Christ's death is universal in its provision, but it is not universal in its application. One is not automatically saved because Christ died, but one is saved when one puts trust in God's gracious provision . . . a person must receive by faith the salvation offered to him or her by the hand of God.[14]

To make sure that we don't misunderstand this great salvation from God, Paul follows up with two "not" statements.

First, "this is not from yourselves, it is the gift of God" (v. 8). What does the word "this" refer to? Although it seems like the word "this" would refer to "faith" since they are close together, it likely does not refer just to faith, because the gender of the pronoun "this" (neuter) does not match the gender of the noun "faith" (feminine). As a result, most scholars take the word "this" to refer to the whole idea of salvation by grace rather than just to the word "faith." The last part of the verse supports this view—"it is the gift of God." God is the origin or source of salvation. There is nothing we have done to generate or create our own rescue.

Second, it is "not by works, so that no one can boast" (v. 9). Salvation is not the result of human initiative (God is the source), nor is it the result of human achievement (God's grace makes the gift possible). The term "works" here in verse 9 refers to human effort or activities aimed at earning God's acceptance: "If I do this or that, God will have to accept me." In Romans and Galatians where Paul is dealing with issues related to Jewish law,

---

[14] Hoehner, *Ephesians*, 341.

he uses the expression "works of law" (Rom. 3:20; Gal. 2:16). In Ephesians with its Gentile context, he simply says "works." Either way, human effort cannot achieve salvation and that helplessness removes all grounds for boasting before God. The word "boast" refers to an attitude of presumption or arrogance before God based on our own accomplishments. The only boast we should make is the boast about what God has done for us through Christ (Gal. 6:14).

Photo 8. *Study group at Pisidian Antioch in modern Turkey—God's workmanship in progress*

So salvation is "by grace" (basis) and "through faith" (means), but what is it for? What is the goal? We are told in verse 10 that we are God's handiwork. God is like an artist producing a masterpiece and we are that masterpiece. God's people are God's greatest work of art. This brings us to the goal of salvation—we have been created in Christ Jesus "to do good works."

There is that word "works" again. Salvation is not "from works" (v. 9), but it is "for good works" (v. 10). How does that work exactly? In the diagram below notice how "works" (or "works of law") attempt to earn or achieve God's acceptance, whereas "good works" flow out of a relationship with God. We don't work for God so much as God works in and through us.

"works of law" or "works" (trying to earn)	$\longrightarrow$	God's acceptance	$\longrightarrow$	"good works" (results from)

We are not saved "by works." Rather, we are saved "by grace through faith." But once we enter a relationship with God through Jesus Christ, we will do good works. True faith will work!

God's Handiwork

> As I think of my Christian life in this world I must stop thinking of it simply in terms of what I do and am doing, but rather think of it in terms of what God is doing to me, that I am in the hands of the great Maker, in the hands of the Creator, and that He is working in me and upon me.[15]

Jesus performed good works (e.g., healing, feeding, casting out demons, teaching, showing compassion) and desires his followers to do the same. The letter of James focuses on the theme of good works. James says that authentic faith demonstrates itself in good works. "Faith without works is dead," James tells us in his letter (2:20, 26). You may be surprised to see how many times the New Testament mentions good works (or doing good). Take some time and look up the verses below on the theme of good works (only a sample). As you give God time to speak to you through his Word, write down your thoughts about how he wants you to live out your faith.

Acts 9:36

2 Corinthians 5:10; 9:8

Galatians 5:6; 6:1–10

---

[15] Lloyd-Jones, *God's Way of Reconciliation*, 143.

Philippians 2:12–13

Colossians 1:9–12

1 Thessalonians 5:12–22

1 Timothy 6:17–19

2 Timothy 2:20–26

Titus 3:8

Hebrews 13:16

James 2:14–26; 3:13

1 Peter 3:8–17; 4:19

In the last part of verse 10 Paul says that God prepared these good works "in advance for us to do." This does not mean that God has already mapped out every good deed you will ever do in life. Rather, God has designed us to walk in good works, to live a life of doing good things. As new creations in Christ we have the capacity to do good for others. God decided in advance or beforehand that this is what he wanted us to do.

So What?

1. How did you explain "by grace through faith" in your own words? What are some ways that people confuse "by grace through faith" and twist this truth into something totally different?

2. How do the two "not" statements help us understand the true meaning of 2:8–9?

3. We are God's handiwork. This means that we have the opportunity to see God's artistry both in ourselves and in other believers. What are some specific ways you've seen this lately?

4. What helps you "work out" your faith without that drifting into "working for" God's acceptance?

5. God created us for good works. As you think about how God has blessed and gifted you as well as the specific needs that you see around you, what are some good works that God might be calling you to live out? (Think about your family, friends, local community, world.)

6. What good works do you think God is calling your church to do?

7

THE CREATION OF A NEW COMMUNITY (PART I)

Ephesians 2:11-18

¹¹ Therefore, remember that formerly you who are Gentiles by birth and called "uncircumcised" by those who call themselves "the circumcision" (which is done in the body by human hands)—¹² remember that at that time you were separate from Christ, excluded from citizenship in Israel and foreigners to the covenants of the promise, without hope and without God in the world. ¹³ But now in Christ Jesus you who once were far away have been brought near by the blood of Christ. ¹⁴ For he himself is our peace, who has made the two groups one and has destroyed the barrier, the dividing wall of hostility, ¹⁵ by setting aside in his flesh the law with its commands and regulations. His purpose was to create in himself one new humanity out of the two, thus making peace, ¹⁶ and in one body to reconcile both of them to God through the cross, by which he put to death their hostility. ¹⁷ He came and preached peace to you who were far away and peace to those who were near. ¹⁸ For through him we both have access to the Father by one Spirit.

This passage (2:11–22) is perhaps the most significant "church" (ecclesiological) section in all the New Testament. It may come as a surprise to realize that this text doesn't give us a long list of commands about how to act. Often when people think of church, they think of a to-do list of duties and obligations, programs and activities. (Are you tired yet?) But that is not how Paul approached church.

In Ephesians 2 we are not presented with a bunch of instructions about how to live like "church" people. The imperatives will come later in Ephesians. There is only one command in the first three chapters of Ephesians and it is found in 2:11: "remember." For now the focus is on what we used to be and how Jesus has changed us. First, we are transformed by God and then we are challenged to live out that change. In essence God is saying to us, "Become who you already are in Christ."

Hyper-activity can cause us to forget who we were before we encountered Jesus. Staying crazily busy can also prevent us from seeing clearly who we now are in Christ. Distractions are one of the devil's chief weapons. Paul challenges his readers to think about who they used to be so that they can appreciate their radical transformation. In the book of Deuteronomy the Israelites were told to remember their slavery in Egypt (Deut. 5:15; 15:15; 16:12; 24:18, 22). In much the same way, when we remember our past slavery to sin and the radical change Jesus has brought, we become more grateful and appreciative for our present life in Christ. Remembering is more than a mental exercise; it prepares us to produce healthy and abundant fruit in our walk with Christ (very different from a life full of hurried religious activity). What are the five things these Gentile Christians were supposed to remember (see v. 12)?

1.

2.

3.

4.

5.

The Ephesian Christians were mostly Gentiles. The word "Gentile" refers to people or nations outside of Israel. The term was used by Jews in the first century in a derogatory fashion to describe anyone who was not a Jew. If you suspect that Jews and Gentiles didn't like each other, you're right. In fact, they generally despised each other (see Acts 22:21–22, e.g.).

The Inner Ring

In December 1944 C. S. Lewis gave a talk to a group of college students about the Inner Ring (see the full essay at http://www.lewissociety.org/innerring.php). In every society there are little groups of people who are on the "inside." Through nicknames, inside jokes, invitations to certain events, particular slang, and the like, some are included while others are excluded. Many people are dominated by the desire to be inside the ring or by the fear of being excluded. Every society needs small groups of people to carry out work or have confidential discussions or solve problems. What is evil is the desire or motivation to be included and to exclude others. Lewis writes, "A thing may be morally neutral and yet the desire for that thing may be dangerous." Getting into the Inner Ring is a lot like peeling an onion in that if you succeed in working through all the additional inner rings, there is nothing left. "Of all the passions," Lewis says, "the passion for the Inner Ring is the most skillful in making a man [or a woman] who is not yet a very bad man do very bad things." Lewis concludes his talk by saying that if you break the desire for the Inner Ring, a surprising result will follow. You "will find that you have come unawares to a real inside: that you are indeed snug and safe at the center of something which, seen from without, would look exactly like an Inner Ring. But the difference is that its secrecy is accidental, and its exclusiveness a by-product." This, Lewis says, is true "friendship" of the sort that honors God.

Talk about a bad memory—no Messiah, no connection to God's people, no promise of salvation, no hope, and no relationship with God. Do you know someone who is desperately disconnected from God and God's people right now? This might be a good time to pray for them once again.

In verse 13 Paul says, "But now in Christ Jesus you who once were far away have been brought near by the blood of Christ." As you read the entire passage, notice the contrasts. There are contrasts in time—"formerly," "at that time," "were" vs. "now." You can also see contrasts in place—"far away" vs. "near." These Gentile Christians used to be separated, alienated, estranged, cut off, and excluded from God and his people. But no longer. Now they have been brought near. They weren't brought near by changing human communities. No, they entered an entirely new kind of community. This new community occurs "in Christ" and is made possible "by the blood of Christ" (a reference to Jesus' sacrificial death on the cross).

The central section of 2:14–18 makes clear how we have been brought near through the work of Christ. It begins by saying that "Jesus is our peace" (v. 14). Where else is "peace" mentioned in this passage?

Jesus is peace, makes peace, and preaches peace. "Peace" refers to wholeness, well-being, security, harmony, and good relationships that God brings about. In Old Testament terms (shalom), peace refers to the way things are supposed to be.

What three things has Jesus done to bring peace (see vv. 14–15)?

1.

2.

3.

Photo 9. An inscription stone from Herod's temple separating Jews and Gentiles. The message reads, "No foreigner [Gentile] is to enter within the fence and enclosure around the temple. Whoever is caught will have himself to blame for his death which will follow." You may recall that Paul was arrested in Jerusalem on charges of bringing Trophimus the Ephesian (a Gentile) into the temple area reserved only for Jews (Acts 21:26–30).

One of the things that Jesus accomplished is illustrated by the stone inscription to the left. While the "dividing wall of hostility" probably refers to Mosaic law (see v. 15), the "death" inscription, as it is called, serves as a vivid reminder of how these two groups hated one another. While the source of the problem is the "in the flesh" for both Jews and Gentiles (v. 11), God's solution is also "in the flesh" (v. 15). God's solution to the "flesh" problem of division was Jesus coming to earth and dying on the cross. Jesus took the very heart of their hatred to the cross and left it there!

What are the two reasons why Jesus removed this hostility by taking it to the cross (vv. 15–16)?

Jesus created something entirely new. Both Jews and Gentiles needed reconciling to God. And as they came into right relationship with God, they also came into right relationship with each other. This reconciliation begins to fulfill God's great plan to unite all things in Christ (1:10). In Christ the walls are torn down and we become "one new humanity" (v. 15) or "one body" (v. 16) with people we formerly hated and despised. Amazing grace indeed!

Peace is now available to those who are "far off" (unrighteous) and to those who are "near" (self-righteous). In our union with the Holy Spirit we now have unhindered access into the presence of the Father because of the death of our Savior Jesus Christ. This is how things are supposed to be.

Reconciliation before Worship

" Therefore, if you are offering your gift at the altar and there remember that your brother or sister has something against you, leave your gift there in front of the altar. First go and be reconciled to them; then come and offer your gift. (Matt. 5:23–24) "

So WHAT?

1. What is significant about Jesus being our peace and not just making peace or preaching peace?

2. How do you suppose "setting aside in his flesh the law with its commands and regulations" helped bring about peace and reconciliation?

3. Since those who are in Christ form one new people, what are some reasons why we occasionally divide into "Inner Rings" even within the body of Christ?

4. Are there relationships in your life where you need to knock down the walls that separate you from other people? What is a small first step you can take to do this?

5. What walls are still standing in your local community? How could the Lord use you and other believers to break down those walls?

8

The Creation of a New Community (Part 2)

Ephesians 2:19-22

19 Consequently, you are no longer foreigners and strangers, but fellow citizens with God's people and also members of his household, 20 built on the foundation of the apostles and prophets, with Christ Jesus himself as the chief cornerstone. 21 In him the whole building is joined together and rises to become a holy temple in the Lord. 22 And in him you too are being built together to become a dwelling in which God lives by his Spirit.

The expression "consequently" in verse 19 indicates that this paragraph is Paul's conclusion to 2:11–22. Using powerful word pictures he spells out the results or consequences of being connected to Christ and to other believers. Paul begins by telling these Gentile Christians that they are "no longer foreigners and strangers." Although these two words mean basically the same thing—"outsiders"—there is some distinction, as Harold Hoehner points out:

> The first is like a tourist traveling in a foreign land which has an agreement with the traveler's land of origin that gives him travel rights. The second is like a person who is legally residing in a foreign country with a residence visa. Neither are citizens nor do they have all the privileges of the citizens in the land.[16]

If you have ever traveled as a tourist or lived as a noncitizen in a foreign country, you can begin to understand how these Gentiles felt. They were outsiders who never truly belonged and never really fit in. But God changed all that in Christ. Although they used to be strangers, foreigners, aliens, outsiders, and so on, now they belonged. This belonging is described in two ways.

---

[16] Hoehner, *Ephesians*, 392.

> *A monolithic church in a multicultural setting is a failure.*[17]

First, they are "fellow citizens with God's people." They are not just citizens, but "fellow citizens with." We find several words in 2:19–22 that emphasize the idea of togetherness: "fellow citizens" (*sympolitēs*), "joined together" (*synarmologeō*), and "built together" (*synoikodomeō*). (The Greek prefix *syn-* often means "with" or "together.") When we are connected to God, we are also connected to God's people, the saints.

Second, they are "members of his household." God does more than make us citizens; he adopts us into his family. Those who are joined to Christ also become part of God's family, members of God's household (see Gal. 6:10). Once they were foreigners and aliens, but now they are citizens and family members. As Kent Hughes puts it, there is something priceless about being part of a family.

> The horizontal relational implications of our being God's family are beautiful. Family is the place where you can be yourself and be assured you are accepted. On Thanksgivings I forgo shaving, put on blue jeans and a flannel shirt, and after dinner lie on the floor and let the grandchildren crawl all over me. Usually I fall asleep. And if things get too hectic, I crawl under our baby grand and sleep where nothing can fall on me. And you know what? Nobody cares! No one says, "What's Dad doing? Where's his tie?" Why? Because we're family, so I can be myself. The Church is the place of reconciliation and acceptance, where you can be your true, redeemed self.[18]

The Ephesian Christians became citizens of God's kingdom and members of God's family because they had been built upon the foundation of the apostles and prophets, with Jesus as the cornerstone (2:20). The same is true for all believers. We are not only citizens and family members; we are also part of God's building, God's temple to be more specific.

In the Old Testament, the temple was the place where God made his presence known. In the New Testament, God's people (both Jews and Gentiles) form a spiritual temple. God once had a temple for his people; now he has his people for a temple. There are three parts to this spiritual temple.

First, there is the foundation. The "apostles and prophets" played a unique, foundational role in the formation of the church. They supplied the bridge to Jesus' life and teachings. They passed on the original

---

[17] Snodgrass, *Ephesians*, 153.

[18] Hughes, *Ephesians*, 99.

Photo 10. *The Western Wall is all that remains of the Jerusalem temple complex that was destroyed by the Romans in AD 70.*

revelation and instruction given by Jesus. The teaching of the New Testament apostles and prophets is the authoritative basis on which the church is founded (see 3:3–6; 1 Cor. 15:1–11). This foundational teaching has been preserved for us in our New Testament Scriptures.

Second, the pride of place in this foundation goes to the cornerstone, Christ Jesus himself. The cornerstone was the most important stone in the building. It was the primary load-bearing stone that determined the dimensions and lines of the rest of the building. All other stones were adjusted to the cornerstone. A temple cornerstone has been discovered in Palestine that weighs about 570 tons.[19] Jesus is the primary foundation stone on which the whole building is constructed. He is THE rock.

Third, the final component of this new temple is the building blocks. Notice how verses 21–22 present parallel ideas:

2:21	2:22
whole building	you too
is joined together and rises to become	are being built together to become
a holy temple	a dwelling in which God lives
in the Lord	by his Spirit

[19] Snodgrass, *Ephesians*, 138.

Once Gentile Christians were not even allowed into the Jerusalem temple. Now they *are* the new temple in Christ. As Peter says, those who follow Christ are like "living stones," being "built into a spiritual house" (1 Pet. 2:5).

The whole building is anchored in Jesus Christ, the cornerstone. The foundational teachings of the New Testament apostles and prophets finish out the foundation. The temple continues to take shape as God lays block upon block. We are not just any building. God is shaping us into a temple. The Jerusalem temple has been replaced by Christ and his followers (cf. Matt. 12:6). God has taken up residence in his people.

> So this is what the Sovereign Lord says: 'See, I lay a stone in Zion, a tested stone, a precious cornerstone for a sure foundation; the one who relies on it will never be stricken with panic.' (Isa. 28:16)

So What?

1. What are some of the privileges of being a citizen of God's kingdom (e.g., refuge, protection, identity, security, etc.)? What about the responsibilities?

2. In our culture where the "normal family" is increasingly rare, how can the church be family for those whose biological families are failing?

3. Are you continuing to build on the right foundation by reading, studying, and reflecting upon the Scriptures on a consistent basis? If so, share with your group what encourages you to connect with God's Word.

4. What is most meaningful to you about the temple analogy—cornerstone, foundation stones, building blocks? Why?

5. What does your church need to do in order to live out 2:11–22 more faithfully?

9

Paul's Unique Role in God's Plan

Ephesians 3:1–13

¹ For this reason I, Paul, the prisoner of Christ Jesus for the sake of you Gentiles— ² Surely you have heard about the administration of God's grace that was given to me for you, ³ that is, the mystery made known to me by revelation, as I have already written briefly. ⁴ In reading this, then, you will be able to understand my insight into the mystery of Christ, ⁵ which was not made known to people in other generations as it has now been revealed by the Spirit to God's holy apostles and prophets. ⁶ This mystery is that through the gospel the Gentiles are heirs together with Israel, members together of one body, and sharers together in the promise in Christ Jesus. ⁷ I became a servant of this gospel by the gift of God's grace given me through the working of his power. ⁸ Although I am less than the least of all the Lord's people, this grace was given me: to preach to the Gentiles the boundless riches of Christ, ⁹ and to make plain to everyone the administration of this mystery, which for ages past was kept hidden in God, who created all things. ¹⁰ His intent was that now, through the church, the manifold wisdom of God should be made known to the rulers and authorities in the heavenly realms, ¹¹ according to his eternal purpose that he accomplished in Christ Jesus our Lord. ¹² In him and through faith in him we may approach God with freedom and confidence. ¹³ I ask you, therefore, not to be discouraged because of my sufferings for you, which are your glory.

Sometimes it is helpful to pause in our journey through Ephesians and look back. After an opening praise to God for all the spiritual blessings "in Christ" (1:3–14) and a prayer that we could truly grasp these blessings (1:15–21), Paul highlights the new life we have in Christ (2:1–10). This new life in Christ creates a new community (2:11–3:21). We tend to think about our faith more as an individual faith (e.g., Christ saved *me*, God has a plan for *my* life), while the Bible emphasizes the corporate or community dimension (*we* are God's people, God has saved *us*). The section on new community plays out in this way:

2:11–22:   Creation of a new community

3:1–13:   Paul's role in God's community plan

3:14–21:   Paul's prayer for the new community

After describing how God desires to unite Jewish and Gentile believers into "one new humanity" (2:15) in Christ, Paul starts to pray for these believers (3:1). Almost immediately, however, he breaks off his prayer to chase an "inspired rabbit." In this digression of 3:2–13 he tells us more about God's "secret plan," or "mystery," and his own role in that plan. Then in 3:14 Paul resumes his prayer.

Paul refers to himself as a "prisoner of Christ Jesus for the sake of you Gentiles" (3:1). How can he say he is a "prisoner of Christ Jesus" when he is really a prisoner of the Roman Empire because of accusations brought by some Jewish religious leaders (he had been arrested in Jerusalem for supposedly bringing a Gentile into the temple—Acts 21:27–32)?

Paul speaks of the "administration of God's grace" given to him (see the grace words in vv. 2, 7, 8). He had been entrusted with a message of life for the Gentiles. If Paul had failed in his responsibility to pass on this message, the Gentiles never would have experienced the grace of God. Grace wasn't just for Paul's personal enjoyment; it was ultimately for the sake of the Gentiles. Grace comes to us, but it also comes through us to others.

This stewardship or responsibility centers upon the "mystery" (a word used in Eph. 1:9; 3:3, 4, 9; 5:32; 6:19). The mystery is God's secret plan to unite Jews and Gentiles as one people in Christ. No human being would have ever discovered or developed this plan. Paul admits that he certainly didn't invent it. Rather, he says that the divine secret came to him "by revelation" (v. 3). On hearing the earlier parts of this letter, the Ephesians would know that God had revealed his plan to Paul (v. 4) at just the right time (v. 5). Outsiders had been accepted into Israel in the past ("other generations"), but not until the coming of Jesus the Messiah and the Holy Spirit at Pentecost would Jews and Gentiles be accepted on equal footing and united into one body in Christ. This plan is brand new. And God chose Paul to make it known to the Gentiles.

The mystery is spelled out in verse 6 using three relational terms to describe these Gentiles. They are "heirs together" of all the blessings God has for his children. They are "members together" of the body of Christ that includes both Jewish and Gentile Christians. And they are "sharers together" of the promise. Again, the mystery is God's plan to have one people in which to live by his Spirit.

God's plan was not only to reveal the mystery to Paul, but also to enlist him in service of that mystery. Paul had become a servant of the gospel by God's grace and power (v. 7). Only God could transform a persecutor of the church into one of the church's great leaders. We experience God's grace and power not only at the beginning of our Christian life, but also throughout the rest of the journey.

> *... last of all he appeared to me also, as to one abnormally born. For I am the least of the apostles and do not even deserve to be called an apostle, because I persecuted the church of God. But by the grace of God I am what I am, and his grace to me was not without effect. No, I worked harder than all of them—yet not I, but the grace of God that was with me. (1 Cor. 15:8–10)*

In thinking about God's grace, Paul is reminded of his own unworthiness (v. 8). Actually, he invents a new form of a Greek word when he calls himself "less than the least" of all the Lord's people. To the superlative ("least"), he adds the comparative ("leaster"). While Paul never downplayed his calling to be an apostle or his missionary ministry, he was deeply aware of his own personal inadequacies. Sometimes we reverse the two—setting aside our service to others and highlighting our own human abilities. Take a moment and read about Paul's calling.

> *I thank Christ Jesus our Lord, who has given me strength, that he considered me trustworthy, appointing me to his service. Even though I was once a blasphemer and a persecutor and a violent man, I was shown mercy because I acted in ignorance and unbelief. The*

> grace of our Lord was poured out on me abundantly, along with the faith and love that are in Christ Jesus. Here is a trustworthy saying that deserves full acceptance: Christ Jesus came into the world to save sinners—of whom I am the worst. But for that very reason I was shown mercy so that in me, the worst of sinners, Christ Jesus might display his immense patience as an example for those who would believe in him and receive eternal life. (1 Tim. 1:12–16) **"**

As you think about Paul's example, in what ways do you desire for God to transform your unworthiness into an avenue for service?

Paul's ministry involved "preaching" to the Gentiles the unfathomable riches of Christ and "making plain" to everyone God's secret plan or mystery (vv. 8–9). Don't miss verse 10. God's larger purpose is to disclose his manifold wisdom to the rulers and authorities through the church. Part of his redemptive plan is to use the church as exhibit #1 to the whole universe.

Did you get that? God's wisdom is "manifold" or "many sided" (i.e., like a diamond). This term was used in the ancient world to describe an intricately embroidered cloth of many colors (e.g., Joseph's coat of many colors in Gen. 37:3) or a multicolored bouquet of flowers. The expression "rulers and authorities" most likely refers to evil spiritual powers (cf. 6:12). Do you see what God is up to? He has brought together in Christ people of every age, color, nation, social class, education level, size, and shape. Through this one people, God is telling the heavenly powers that their authority has been broken. The walls are down, the barriers have been destroyed. God's master plan is taking shape, and there is nothing they can do to stop it.

We cannot be part of God's community apart from Jesus Christ, but we also cannot be connected to Christ without being joined to God's community. (We neglect our local community to our own spiritual detriment.)

God has a cosmic purpose for his one multicultural, multifaceted church—to announce his wisdom to the heavenly powers. Again, we are God's message board to the universe.

Photo 11. *Like a beautiful silk carpet woven from threads of various colors, God's manifold community displays his wise and amazing purpose.*

God's good purpose is being accomplished in Christ (v. 11). Through faith—whether our faith in Christ or Christ's faithfulness or both—we have "freedom and confidence" to approach God (v. 12; cf. Heb. 4:16). All believers are priests. No hostile power, seen or unseen, can limit our access to our heavenly Father. We may come into his presence confidently, without fear. We may speak freely and openly. We may be candid, even bold. We have nothing to hide, nothing to conceal. The Judge is our Father.

In verse 13 Paul supplies the "therefore" conclusion to the statement back in verse 2—"surely you have heard about the administration of God's grace that was given to me for you . . . therefore, do not be discouraged because of my sufferings for you." Don't lose heart, Paul says, because my suffering is "your glory." Paul's tribulations actually honored, exalted, and benefited the Gentiles.

So What?

1. As you reflect on our study of Ephesians up to this point, what has
   been the most life-changing truth you have learned?

2. Complete the following sentence about your own life and then explain your answers: "I am a prisoner of _____ for
   the sake of _____."

3. Has there been a time when you were keenly aware that God's grace
   was moving through you for the sake of other people? Share that
   experience with your group.

4. Paul may have downplayed his human abilities, but he never downplayed his calling as an apostle. What are some challenges we face as we attempt to follow his example in this area?

5. Since God desires to create a "manifold" church, what practical steps can your church take to look more like what God had in mind?

6. What connections do you see between suffering and glory? What might this mean for you personally or for your church?

10

PAUL'S PRAYER FOR THE NEW COMMUNITY

Ephesians 3:14-21

14 For this reason I kneel before the Father, 15 from whom every family in heaven and on earth derives its name. 16 I pray that out of his glorious riches he may strengthen you with power through his Spirit in your inner being, 17 so that Christ may dwell in your hearts through faith. And I pray that you, being rooted and established in love, 18 may have power, together with all the Lord's holy people, to grasp how wide and long and high and deep is the love of Christ, 19 and to know this love that surpasses knowledge—that you may be filled to the measure of all the fullness of God. 20 Now to him who is able to do immeasurably more than all we ask or imagine, according to his power that is at work within us, 21 to him be glory in the church and in Christ Jesus throughout all generations, for ever and ever! Amen.

Paul had started to pray in 3:1 ("for this reason"), before digressing in 3:2–13 to talk about his own role in God's amazing plan to unite Jews and Gentiles in Christ. Now he returns to prayer. His "reason" for praying (v. 14) goes back to the new life and new community described in Ephesians 2. Take a moment and read Ephesians 2 again and summarize what God has done for us in Christ. (It's always good to rehearse what God has done.)

This is not the first time that Paul has prayed in Ephesians. In 1:15–23 he prayed that God would help us comprehend and experience all the blessings we have received from God. Specifically, Paul asks that we would know the hope of God's calling (past), the glory of God's inheritance (future), and the greatness of God's power (present). Paul's second prayer in 3:14–21 is organized into three parts—the introduction to the prayer (vv. 14–15), the prayer itself (vv. 16–19), and the doxology (vv. 20–21).

In the introduction he speaks of "kneeling." One day every knee will bow in reverence to God (Isa. 45:23; Phil. 2:10), but the kneeling has already begun among the followers of Jesus (3:14). Our word "kneel" translates the expression "bend my knees," an idiom for prayer, where the posture itself signifies the act of submission, worship, and prayer. Paul makes a play on words when he mentions kneeling before the Father (*patēr*) from whom every "family" (*patria*) is named. As the "Name-Giver," God is the sovereign Creator and Sustainer of the universe.

Photo 12. *Model of Jerusalem temple*

Even though he is in prison, Paul can still pray. No matter what our circumstances, we can still pray. As we pray, we approach the Father with "freedom and confidence" (3:12), yet we also "bow our knees" before the Father who is Creator of all and is able to do far beyond all that we ask or imagine (3:14–15, 20). Our Father is both loving and holy, both merciful and mighty. As you approach God in prayer, are you able to appreciate equally both aspects of his character, or do you tend to favor one aspect and ignore the other?

The main request of Paul's prayer is found in verse 16: "I pray that . . . he [God] may strengthen you." That sounds good, but what does it mean? Paul's train of thought in this section gets a bit complicated. Perhaps a question-and-answer format will help us understand what he is saying:

Q   What is God's standard of granting us strength?

A   God will give us strength "out of his glorious riches" (3:16). Perhaps an even better translation is that God gives us strength "according to" or "corresponding to" the wealth of his glory (i.e., his essential being of radiance and power). There can be no higher standard of giving.

Q   What kind of strength does God give?

A   First, God gives us "inner" strength (3:16). This relates to the heart or mind of the believer (in contrast to outer, physical strength). Second, this strength comes to us through God's Holy Spirit.

Q   How will we know when God has answered this prayer for strength?

A   When Christ is at home in our hearts (3:17). The word "dwell" means "to live, to reside, to settle down." When God the Father grants us strength through the work of his Spirit, Christ will settle down and be at home in the very center of our lives. This is not referring to Christ's indwelling that begins at conversion, but to his ongoing fellowship with believers. To get a better understanding, think of the opposite. What if we do not turn to God for spiritual strength and find ourselves out of fellowship with God? The result is that our hearts begin to grow cold and hard and Christ becomes unwelcome or uncomfortable with us. A good illustration of what God desires is found in Revelation 3:20 (spoken to believers by Jesus): "Here I am! I stand at the door and knock. If anyone hears my voice and opens the door, I will come in and eat with that person, and they with me." When we are strengthened with God's strength, Christ will be perfectly at home in our hearts. Our fellowship with Jesus will be sweet.

Q   Why does Christ desire to dwell in our hearts?

A   The purpose of Christ being at home in our hearts is so that we may experience his love even more. Because we have already been "rooted and established in love," we are ready to know Christ's love at an even deeper level. Paul uses two metaphors here—our roots go down deep into the soil of God's love (agricultural) and our lives are built upon the foundation of God's love (architectural).

We already know God's love, but he wants us to know his love even more. God's love is both the starting point and the finish line.

Q   What is the place where we comprehend Christ's love?

A   We comprehend Christ's love "with all the Lord's holy people." In other words, we understand and experience Christ's love in the context of Christian community. Love means doing what is best for the loved one and this can only happen as we live life together.

Q   How is Christ's love described?

A   Actually there is no object for the verb "grasp" in 3:18. Paul does say that this unspecified object has four dimensions: it is wide, long, high, and deep. Most interpreters see verse 19 as explaining verse 18, where Paul clearly speaks of the love of Christ as the main topic. The paradox is that we are called to know Christ's vast love that "surpasses knowledge." No matter how much we know of Christ's love, there will always be more to know and experience. We will never come to the end of Christ's love; it's just too big!

The Four Magnitudes of Love

Wide enough to embrace the world (John 3:16)

Long enough to last forever (1 Cor. 13:8)

High enough to take sinners to heaven (1 John 3:1–2)

Deep enough to send Christ to earth (Phil. 2:8)[20]

Q   What is the goal or final purpose of Paul's prayer?

A   That we will "be filled to the measure of all the fullness of God" (v. 19). In this context, the "fullness of God" and the love of Christ are closely connected. When we know the love of Christ that surpasses knowledge, we are filled with the fullness of God.

In verse 19 does Paul go too far and ask for too much? We might think so, until we read the doxology in 3:20–21. We pray to the God who "is able to do immeasurably more than all we ask or imagine." Praise his name! The word "able" is the same word translated "power" in 3:16. God

---

[20] Hughes, *Ephesians*, 117.

is the powerful One who is not limited by our enormous requests or our stagnant imaginations. He is "able" (powerful) to do infinitely more than whatever we can ask or think.

To give God glory is not to add to God's character, but rather to acknowledge God's fame, honor, radiance, and splendor. God is to be praised "in the church and in Christ Jesus"—the only time these two phrases appear together in a doxology. God's glory is made known in Christ, but also in the community of Christ. We are God's masterpiece of grace for all to see. There will be no end to ascribing glory to God. Our praise begins now ("throughout all generations") and continues throughout eternity ("for ever and ever"). Spontaneously we respond "Amen." This is true! This is real!

So What?

1. Our view of God influences how we pray. How does this passage help you see God the way he really is so that you can pray more effectively?

2. How does Christ being at home in our hearts relate to living in God's strength?

3. What does it mean to you that we comprehend Christ's love in the context of community?

4. This passage deals a lot with the love of Christ. Right now in your life, how are you experiencing the love of Christ or what are you learning about his love?

5. We typically pray for others to experience physical strength, while Paul's prayer is all about inner, spiritual strength. What's up with that?

6. What part of this prayer do you most need someone to pray for you?

II

NEW WALK IN UNITY (PART I)

Ephesians 4:1–6

> [1] *As a prisoner for the Lord, then, I urge you to live a life worthy of the calling you have received.* [2] *Be completely humble and gentle; be patient, bearing with one another in love.* [3] *Make every effort to keep the unity of the Spirit through the bond of peace.* [4] *There is one body and one Spirit, just as you were called to one hope when you were called;* [5] *one Lord, one faith, one baptism;* [6] *one God and Father of all, who is over all and through all and in all.*

In the first three chapters of Ephesians Paul explained God's magnificent plan. Through Jesus Christ, who died on the cross and was raised from the dead, God has offered *new life* to individuals (2:1–10) and created a *new community* of those who are connected to Christ (2:11–3:21). God has done amazing things to rescue us from our sinfulness and restore us to himself. But God cares about more than just "saving souls." He cares about how we live right now in this world.

As a result, the rest of the letter concentrates on our *new walk*. Now that we have a new relationship with God and enjoy life in a new community, how should we live? Ephesians 1–3 is more theological, while Ephesians 4–6 is more practical. Without sound theology, our "practice" becomes confusing, disoriented, and self-centered. But without authentic practice, our "theology" becomes cold, narrow, boring, and equally self-focused.

In 4:1 the word "then" ("therefore" in many translations) tells us that our practice should be based upon sound theology. We should live according to God's reality. Both theology and practice are equally important and should never be separated. God calls us to live out what we have experienced in him. Our obedience always comes as a response to his grace. New life brings us into new community and encourages a new walk, all to the glory of God. The rest of Ephesians looks like this:

4:1–6:20	New Walk in Christ
4:1–16	Walk in Unity
4:17–32	Walk in Holiness
5:1–6	Walk in Love
5:7–14	Walk in Light
5:15–6:9	Walk in Wisdom
6:10–20	Walk in Strength
6:21–24	Conclusion to the Letter

In 4:1–6 Paul urges believers to embrace the unity they already have (vv. 1–3) and then illustrates how the Triune God serves as the basis of our unity (vv. 4–6). Paul's exhortation carries both urgency and authority. The word "live" (or "walk") refers to the conduct, or lifestyle, of the believer. Paul urges believers to live "worthy of the calling." (The "calling" is not talking about a professional ministry position, but about the call to follow Jesus.) We also shouldn't miss the fact that Paul writes as a "prisoner for the Lord." He doesn't want the Ephesians to worry about his imprisonment (3:13), but he is concerned about how they are living while he is in prison (4:1). His own sacrificial commitment stands behind his words. We are much more willing to listen to leaders when they are living out the vision themselves in sacrificial ways.

Jesus didn't just call us to salvation. The Christian life is about much more than "getting saved" so that we can have our sins forgiven and go to heaven when we die. Those are definitely important, but Jesus also calls us to live now in a way that is worthy of our new relationship with God. The next few verses (as well as the next three chapters) spell out what a life worthy of the calling looks like. Are you surprised that it all starts with unity?

A Worthy Walk Is God-Centered

" The God-centered focus of mission turns inside-out our obsession with mission plans, agendas, goals, strategies, and grand schemes. We ask, 'Where does God fit into the story of my life?' when the real question is 'Where does my life fit into the great story of God's mission?' . . . I may wonder what kind of mission God has for me, when I should ask what kind of me God wants for his mission.[21] "

---

[21] Christopher J. H. Wright, "Upside-Down World."

In 4:2 there are four qualities that characterize the worthy walk—humility, gentleness, patience, and loving forbearance. Humility is essential to unity. In the ancient world humility was not considered a virtue, but despised as a weakness. But Jesus valued this "lowliness of mind" (see Phil. 2:1–11). Pride leads to power struggles, conflict, and disunity, while humility promotes the good of the community. Humble people have a realistic understanding of who they are plus they see the value and worth of others.

Gentleness ("meekness") nurtures and considers others rather than being harsh, dominant, rough, or retaliatory. The gentle person sees other people as important, even fragile, and handles them with care. Gentleness bears burdens (Gal. 6:1–2). This quality should not be confused with weakness or lack of conviction (cf. Jesus in Matt. 11:29). A gentle person is actually a strong person who has chosen to control that strength and use it to serve others.

Patience is the quality of being able to put up with the faults and failures of others. We are patient when we make allowances for people who are aggravating, annoying, difficult, and even offensive.

Bearing with one another in love is closely related to patience. Rather than flying into a rage or retaliating, we must do all we can to maintain right relationships. Our attitude in the midst of this endurance should be one of love. Practically speaking, this may mean that we let some things go, we back off from judging, and we resist the urge to focus on faults.

In most local churches there are huge differences among the people. Unity is not easy to maintain, but unity is extremely important to God and pleases him greatly! Humility, gentleness, patience, and loving forbearance are not passive qualities. We have to be intentional and diligent in allowing the Lord to work these qualities into our lives. In fact, Paul makes this very point in 4:3 where he instructs us to "make every effort to keep the unity of the Spirit through the bond of peace." This word translated "make every effort" carries the idea of working with determination even when the task is difficult. Maintaining unity is not something that happens automatically or effortlessly. We must work hard to preserve unity. Preserving unity demands a wholehearted effort from the whole person.

You know what is super encouraging? We don't have to create unity; we only have to keep or preserve or protect a unity that has already been created by the Lord. God has already accomplished our unity in Christ and made it available through his Spirit. We are already family members! Our task is to avoid destroying the unity we have been given in Christ. We are called to work hard to maintain unity. We should remember that "unity is not the goal; unity *in Christ* is, . . . Therefore, there are limits to unity. The church and its unity are always Christologically defined."[22]

---

[22] Snodgrass, *Ephesians*, 221.

The unity of the Spirit exists in the bond of peace. As we live in peace with each other rather than in tension and conflict, peace acts like a glue that cements our oneness and unity.

The word "one" is used seven times in verses 4–6. Our unity as the church is based upon the unity within the Trinity. There is one body—one universal church. All Christians are related to each other. There are not multiple "bodies of Christ" in different locations, but one body of Christ with each local congregation representing that body. This oneness of body, however, must be made real and visible in each local gathering of believers. This takes us back to diligence in preserving unity. The one Spirit creates and promotes unity. We are members of one body because we possess the Spirit of God (1 Cor. 12:13; Rom. 8:9). The Spirit is not responsible for splits, factions, disharmony, and division. Those come from other, anti-God sources.

We have been called to one hope of our calling. We are people of hope. Our hope is more than wishful thinking (i.e., "I hope it doesn't rain"). A Christian's hope is the absolute certainty that God will work out his plan and keep his promises. The story we share has the same ending, an ending filled with hope.

There is one Lord. "Lord" was a title for Yahweh in the Old Testament, a title the early Christians applied to Jesus. The common confession of all Christians is "Jesus is Lord" (Rom. 10:9; 1 Cor. 8:6; 12:3). The expression "one faith" probably refers both to our personal trust in Christ and to the object of that trust—our common set of beliefs (see 4:13; Jude 3, 20). There is also "one baptism." In the early church water baptism held great importance and was closely connected to faith in Christ (Acts 2:38; 8:16, 35–39; 19:5; 1 Cor. 1:13–15). Baptism is the public rite of initiation that Jesus commanded his followers to practice (Matt. 28:19–20).

Paul completes 4:1–6 with a statement about the "one God and Father of all." The one God is "over all," pointing to his transcendence, sovereignty, and power. He is high and lifted up. But God is also "through all and in all," meaning that he is intimately and actively present through his Spirit. He is near and close.

SO WHAT?

1. What happens when we try to separate theology from practice (e.g., people are given a bunch of rules, but no reasons why God gives us those rules)? What encourages you to keep theology and practice connected?

2. Why do you suppose that Paul begins the practical portion of his letter by focusing on unity?

3. Of the four qualities mentioned in 4:2, which one do you need to develop even more in your life? Any ideas about how that can happen?

4. Does it make any difference to know that we don't have to create or establish unity, but only protect and maintain unity?

5. As you think about the seven affirmations of "oneness" in 4:4–6, how do these influence your understanding of unity? Is Paul advocating unity at any price? Why or why not?

6. What do you see as the greatest obstacle to preserving unity in your church? What about the greatest encouragement to maintaining unity?

12

New Walk in Unity (Part 2)

Ephesians 4:7-16

[7] But to each one of us grace has been given as Christ apportioned it. [8] This is why it says: "When he ascended on high, he took many captives and gave gifts to his people." [9] (What does "he ascended" mean except that he also descended to the lower, earthly regions? [10] He who descended is the very one who ascended higher than all the heavens, in order to fill the whole universe.) [11] So Christ himself gave the apostles, the prophets, the evangelists, the pastors and teachers, [12] to equip his people for works of service, so that the body of Christ may be built up [13] until we all reach unity in the faith and in the knowledge of the Son of God and become mature, attaining to the whole measure of the fullness of Christ. [14] Then we will no longer be infants, tossed back and forth by the waves, and blown here and there by every wind of teaching and by the cunning and craftiness of people in their deceitful scheming. [15] Instead, speaking the truth in love, we will grow to become in every respect the mature body of him who is the head, that is, Christ. [16] From him the whole body, joined and held together by every supporting ligament, grows and builds itself up in love, as each part does its work.

Although 4:1–6 makes it clear that there is one Lord and one body, this unity should not be seen as boring, lifeless, mechanical uniformity. As John Stott puts it, "We are not to imagine that every Christian is an exact replica of every other, as if we had all been mass-produced in some celestial factory."[23] In 4:7–16 we see that diversity within the body of Christ actually enriches unity. When people exercise their different gifts and fulfill their various ministries, the one body grows and matures in love. As strange as it may seem, the Lord wants to use our differences to make us even more unified.

---

[23] Stott, *Ephesians*, 155.

Each follower of Christ has been given "grace" (v. 7). In this context "grace" probably refers to a grace gift or spiritual gift—a God-given ability to serve. These gifts are given to "each one," but in different proportions—"as Christ apportioned it" (cf. Rom. 12:3; 1 Cor. 12:11). Jesus determines how we are gifted and the extent or capacity of our gifting.

In 4:8–9 Paul quotes Psalm 68:18 to confirm what he has just said about gifts. In this Psalm, God is pictured as a triumphant warrior marching up Mount Zion leading a defeated enemy after him. The victorious king would receive gifts from his enemies and distribute the spoils of war to his army and his people. Paul uses this picture from the Old Testament to verify that Christ has defeated his enemies, has ascended, and now has given gifts to his people.

In verses 9–10, Christ's "descent" probably refers to his incarnation (his coming to earth as a man) and even to his death and burial. (It is very unlikely that this refers to a descent to Hades.) By coming to earth and dying on the cross ("descent") and by his resurrection from the dead and his ascension, Christ defeated Satan, sin, and death. From this exalted position "higher than all the heavens," he is able to "fill the whole universe" (v. 10), meaning that he exercises his lordship over everything and that includes giving gifts to his people.

We read in 4:11 of spiritual gifts that Christ gives his church—"the apostles, the prophets, the evangelists, the pastors and teachers." There are five lists of spiritual gifts in the New Testament—Romans 12:6–8; 1 Corinthians 12:8–10, 28–30; Ephesians 4:11; 1 Peter 4:10–11. Each list is different from the others. No single list contains all the gifts. Each list illustrates the kinds of gifts that Christ gives to his people. What you may notice is that in Ephesians 4 the gifts are actually people—gifted people.

How Many Ministers Are in Your Church?

Watch out for trick questions. Ephesians 4:12 shows us that God gives gifted people to his church not to *be* the ministers, but to *equip* or prepare the ministers. Every Christian is a minister or servant. How many? A lot more than most people think.

As we saw in 2:20, the apostles and prophets played a unique, foundational role in the formation of the church. They supplied the bridge from Jesus' life and teachings to the later church. They passed on the original revelation and instruction given by Jesus. The teaching of the New Testament apostles and prophets is the authoritative basis on which the church is founded. This foundational teaching has been preserved for us in our New Testament Scriptures. Apostles and prophets exist today only in a secondary sense of pioneer missionaries or church planters (apostles or sent ones) or the ability to apply with special insight and power the truths of Scripture to the contemporary situation (prophets).

While all Christians are charged with making disciples (Matt. 28:18–20), an evangelist is one who is especially skilled in making the gospel clear and convincing to unbelievers. Some interpreters think the phrase "pastors and teachers" refers to the same group (because one definite article governs both nouns in Greek). This would suggest that all pastors will be teachers and that all teachers will be pastors. But Greek grammarian Dan Wallace points out that since both nouns are plural, it is extremely unlikely that they refer to the same group—closely related perhaps, but not identical.[24] As most commentators conclude, this means that all pastors will be teachers, but not all teachers will be pastors.

Pastors (shepherds) nurture and care for people through encouraging, counseling, exhorting, guiding, and administering the activities in the local congregation. Teachers explain and apply the Scriptures so that people are instructed in sound doctrine and challenged to live out what they are learning.

Christ has given these gifted people to his church for an extremely significant purpose—"to equip his people for works of service, so that the body of Christ may be built up" (4:12). In his book, *Love Your God with All Your Mind*, Christian theologian and philosopher J. P. Moreland says it well:

> Their [pastors and teachers] job description is to equip others for ministry, not to do the ministry themselves and have others come and passively support them. . . . The senior pastor model tends to centralize ministry around the church building and the pastor himself. Where he is, is where the action is. We bring people to him to evangelize, to counsel, and so forth. On this view, there is little need actually to equip parishioners to develop their own gifts, talents, and ministries because their job is to support the minister. But according to Ephesians 4, this tradition has it backwards. New Testament ministry is decentralized, and the function of the pastors-teachers is to equip others to do the ministry. If we were more serious about this approach, we would do a better job of providing theological, biblical, philosophical, psychological, and other forms of training in our churches because without it, the ministers (that is, the members of the church) would not be adequately equipped to do the ministry.[25]

When these gifted leaders "equip" believers, they prepare or train them by giving them the knowledge and skills necessary to minister or serve effectively. Paul rejects the idea of letting the "professionals" do the ministry. Instead, God's "gifts" to the church are supposed to prepare the rest of us for "works of service" (v. 12). This ties back to 4:7, where we saw that

---

24 Wallace, *Exegetical Syntax*, 284.

25 Moreland, *Love Your God with All Your Mind*, 191.

each person has been gifted by God. The goal of it all is to build up the body of Christ (v. 12).

Photo 13. *An ancient Odeon (or Odeum) was a covered meeting hall used also for concerts. This particular Odeon is in Ephesus. In many ways the church should be like a symphony orchestra. When we play independently, the result is unbearable, brain-crushing noise. We cover our ears. But when our different instruments (or gifts) are unified around the Composer's creation and the Conductor's direction, the resulting music is indescribably beautiful.*

In 4:13–16 we come back full circle to the theme of unity and where unity is leading us. The aim of all this "body building" through the exercise of gifts is maturity. We are to continue serving "until" . . . (v. 13). Until when? Until we attain a unity that is mature.

What does a mature unity look like? A mature unity is a unity of "the faith" (a common set of beliefs centered on Christ) and unity of "the knowledge of the Son of God" (both informational and relational, both knowing facts and knowing a Person). A mature unity means nothing less than "attaining to the whole measure of the fullness of Christ" (v. 13). We continue using our gifts to build the body until we become like Christ. In case you were wondering, the church will not measure up to Christ's stature this side of heaven. We can, however, move in that direction.

The more immediate goal has both negative (4:14) and positive (4:15–16) aspects. Growing toward maturity means we should stop letting cunning, deceitful people trick us through any kind of unreliable teaching. We are supposed to have a childlike faith (Matt. 19:14), but not a childish gullibility, a susceptible faith. Children can be easily influenced by others, like a small wave in a huge ocean. That's not for us. Instead, we are to grow to become like Christ, by "speaking the truth in love" (v. 15). Many translations have "speaking the truth," but in the original it simply says "truthing in love." This suggests that believers should be truthful, transparent, and real not just in what we say but also in how we live, without any hint of cunning or deceit. And we should live truth with an attitude of love. As the head of the body, Christ joins us together and holds us there. We are connected like the joints and ligaments of a human body. As each (gifted) person does her or his God-given job, the whole body grows in love.

So What?

1. What do you think about the analogy of an orchestra to illustrate how diversity actually strengthens unity? Can you think of a better one?

2. How do you see yourself gifted to build up the body of Christ? How do you see the people in your group gifted?

3. Why do you suppose there is such a strong emphasis on "building the body of Christ" rather than "evangelizing the lost" in this passage and in all of Ephesians?

4. How well do you think "every-member ministry" is working in your church? Any advice for the leaders about how to be more effective in "equipping the saints"? Any advice for the "saints"?

5. John Stott says, "Truth becomes hard if it is not softened by love; love becomes soft if it is not strengthened by truth."[26] Talk about your struggles and successes in holding together truth and love.

---

[26] Stott, *Ephesians*, 172.

13

NEW WALK IN HOLINESS (PART I)

Ephesians 4:17-24

[17] So I tell you this, and insist on it in the Lord, that you must no longer live as the Gentiles do, in the futility of their thinking. [18] They are darkened in their understanding and separated from the life of God because of the ignorance that is in them due to the hardening of their hearts. [19] Having lost all sensitivity, they have given themselves over to sensuality so as to indulge in every kind of impurity, and they are full of greed. [20] That, however, is not the way of life you learned [21] when you heard about Christ and were taught in him in accordance with the truth that is in Jesus. [22] You were taught, with regard to your former way of life, to put off your old self, which is being corrupted by its deceitful desires; [23] to be made new in the attitude of your minds; [24] and to put on the new self, created to be like God in true righteousness and holiness.

In the first part of Ephesians 4 we learned what it means to walk in unity. Great stuff. Beginning in 4:17, Paul starts a new section, again using the word "live" or "walk" (a metaphor denoting a person's way of life). Now that we are unified and together, we need to be together for the right reasons, going in the right direction. In this chapter we focus on walking in holiness. Our passage consists of two parts. What is the basic idea of 4:17–19?

What about the main idea of 4:20–24?

If you noticed the shift from a negative description of how the Gentiles behave to a positive picture of how followers of Christ ought to live, you nailed it. In fact, this passage is filled with contrasts between the old life in paganism and the new life in Christ. Look in 4:17–24 above for the positive replacements (stated or implied) to the negative items listed in the chart below.

Old Life in Paganism	New Life in Christ
Former Gentile life (v. 17)	
Futile thinking (v. 17)	
Darkened understanding (v. 18)	
Separated from the life of God (v. 18)	
Ignorance within (v. 18)	
Hardness of hearts (v. 18)	
Without sensitivity (v. 19)	
Given over to sensuality (v. 19)	
Indulgence in impurity (v. 19)	
Greediness (v. 19)	

We know that Paul's words are both important and urgent because of his introduction: "So I tell you this, and insist on it in the Lord." He's serious. He exhorts his readers (and us) not to "live as the Gentiles do." He is using "Gentiles" not in an ethnic sense, but in a moral sense. Although the readers were ethnic Gentiles (rather than Jews) and could never change that, they could live differently in a moral sense. To live like a Gentile morally meant to live an ungodly life. Paul commands these believers to no longer live in this way, implying that at one time they did live an ungodly lifestyle. This former life in paganism was characterized by distorted thinking that resulted in ungodly behavior.

Photo 14. *Ephesus was home to the temple of Artemis, the goddess of fertility, who was often portrayed as a many-breasted figure (see photo on page 4). The worship of Artemis involved not only idolatry, but also sensuality and immorality.*

Write out all the phrases in verses 18–19 that describe the mental malfunction of a person without Christ:

The term "futility" in verse 17 refers to a worthlessness or emptiness. Their reasoning process is clouded or darkened. They are separated from real life that comes only from God. This separation is caused by their ignorance—not an innocent ignorance or lack of information, but a willful and stubborn refusal to acknowledge God. Ignorance of God means blatantly ignoring God. Such ignorance comes from within due to one's hardness of heart. The heart is "the center of a person, the seat of thought and understanding, will or volition, and, as here, of religious and moral conduct."[27]

---

[27] Hoehner, *Ephesians*, 588.

They had become "callous"—a term that could refer to callous skin that no longer has feeling. Because they had lost any sense of shame or embarrassment, they began to indulge their sensual appetites. There is no evidence that these Gentiles ever felt remorse or regret for their wicked behavior. Instead, they abandoned themselves to "every kind of impurity." Klyne Snodgrass writes, "As in Romans 1:21–32, the loss of relation to God leads to uncontrolled, outrageous, sinful behavior, especially with regard to sexuality."[28] Greediness suggests that the pagan lifestyle included an unquenchable thirst for more immoral experiences. Romans 1 also teaches that God gives people over to the enslaving sin that they have already freely chosen. Sin carries its own devastating consequence.

The Progress of Corruption

Dispositions and acts form character, which then forms dispositions and acts. A mere state of mind can eventually swell to become a person's destiny. . . : sow a thought, and reap a deed; sow a deed, and reap another deed; sow some deeds, and reap a habit; sow some habits, and reap a character.[29]

No wonder that Paul urges these Christians not to walk as the Gentiles walk. We were created to pursue something, however, so what should we pursue with all of our heart and soul? Let's look at the positive replacement in 4:20–24.

We are not to live like Gentiles, because we did not learn Christ in this way. Nowhere else in the Greek Bible do we find this image of "learning a person." This is more than factual learning. They had "heard about" and "were taught" in Jesus. He is the teacher, the content, and the atmosphere of the teaching. Truth is not portrayed here as vague, ambiguous, or abstract. The living person of Jesus embodies the truth! Since they had been educated in the person of Jesus Christ himself, they knew better than to revert back to their futile, darkened, isolated, ignorant, hard-hearted, callous, indecent, impure, and greedy existence. They had experienced life. Why go back to death?

---

28 Snodgrass, *Ephesians*, 231.

29 Plantinga, *Not the Way*, 70.

Christ be with me, Christ within me, Christ behind me, Christ before me, Christ beside me, Christ to win me, Christ to comfort and restore me, Christ beneath me, Christ above me, Christ in quiet, Christ in danger, Christ in hearts of all that love me, Christ in mouth of friend and stranger.

—From St. Patrick's Lorica
or "Breastplate" (protection) Prayer, 5th century

In 4:20–21 we see that believers have "learned" Christ. In verses 22–24 Paul spells out the details of our education in Christ. It's important to see how this section is organized so that we can apply it correctly [my own translation below]:

> You "were taught" (past tense) . . .
>
> 22: that you have put off (past tense) the old man who is being corrupted by deceitful desires
>
> 23: that you are being renewed (present tense) in the spirit of your mind
>
> 24: that you have put on (past tense) the new man who has been created in God's image

Instead of 4:22–24 giving us a new set of imperatives (commands to "put off" the old and "put on" the new), it is better to see these as statements of fact (indicative) about what has already happened in our lives at conversion.[30] We are being reminded that when we became Christians, we laid aside the old person and became a new person. The parallel passage in Colossians 3:9–10 makes it clear: "Do not lie to each other, since you have taken off your old self with its practices and have put on the new self, which is being renewed in knowledge in the image of its Creator." The "old man" is the human being without God (see vv. 17–19). The "new man" is the human being who has been recreated in God's image in Christ.

God is calling us to behave and live like the new people we already are in Christ! We have a new identity, both as a community (2:15; 4:13, 16) and as individuals (4:7, 11, 12, 16). The Lord is not commanding us to become something we're not or to behave our way into a new state of being. Rather he recreates us in Christ, makes us new people, gives us a brand new identity, and then says, "Be who you already are in Christ!"

---

[30] So Hoehner, *Ephesians*, 600–602.

There is a present-tense (ongoing action) part to this new life that we shouldn't miss. In 4:23 we are to "be made new in the attitude of your minds" (cf. Rom. 12:1–2; Phil. 4:8–9). As we continually allow the Holy Spirit to renew our minds, we will be continually transformed into Christ's likeness. A definite change has taken place, but we still must give God space to work in our lives.

So What?

1. Why do you suppose Paul places such an emphasis on the mind in this passage, both negatively and positively?

2. Do you think that Paul's description of the Gentile lifestyle in 4:17–19 is too harsh? How does it help to know that he is rejecting the Gentiles' sinful way of life rather than rejecting their worth or value as persons created in God's image?

3. Why are believers "prone to wander"? Why do we sometimes want to revert back to the old life even though we know it leads only death?

4. Do you find the metaphor of "learning Christ" helpful or not? Why?

5. At conversion we were given a completely new identity and subsequently asked to live out that new identity (be who you already are). Why do Christians struggle so much to believe that they really are new creatures in Christ, that they really do have a new identity?

6. What are some specific habits that we can practice to allow the Spirit to renew our minds? Get beyond pat answers to specific, targeted ways of letting God shape your thinking. Also, consider thought practices to avoid as well as those to embrace.

14

New Walk in Holiness (Part 2)

Ephesians 4:25–32

25 Therefore each of you must put off falsehood and speak truthfully to your neighbor, for we are all members of one body. 26 "In your anger do not sin": Do not let the sun go down while you are still angry, 27 and do not give the devil a foothold. 28 Anyone who has been stealing must steal no longer, but must work, doing something useful with their own hands, that they may have something to share with those in need. 29 Do not let any unwholesome talk come out of your mouths, but only what is helpful for building others up according to their needs, that it may benefit those who listen. 30 And do not grieve the Holy Spirit of God, with whom you were sealed for the day of redemption. 31 Get rid of all bitterness, rage and anger, brawling and slander, along with every form of malice. 32 Be kind and compassionate to one another, forgiving each other, just as in Christ God forgave you.

We have put off the old person and put on the new person in Christ. Because we are new people living as part of a new community, God calls us to a new lifestyle. He knows we need practical instructions, however, so we are taught in 4:17–24 and 4:25–32 what it means to walk in holiness. Because God is holy, he is sensitive to anything unholy in our lives. Remember, this new person has been "created to be like God in true righteousness and holiness" (4:23).

If you like practical teaching that you can apply to your life, here you have it. Make a short list of all the topics covered in this section (e.g., truth, anger):

Notice also how the whole passage is organized. There are five exhortations: verses 25, 26–27, 28, 29–30, and 31–32. Each exhortation or challenge has three parts: (1) a negative command, (2) a positive command, and (3) the reason for the positive command. There are slight adjustments throughout, but the overall pattern holds and shows a strong contrast between what helps community and what hurts it. You may want to take time to circle the positive commands, put a box around the negative commands, and underline the reasons for the commands in the text above.

Lying (or deceit of any kind) has no place in the life of the Christian or in the Christian community. What can we learn from the following verses about lying?

- John 8:44

- Romans 1:25

- 2 Thessalonians 2:9–12

- 1 Timothy 4:1–2

- 1 John 2:21, 27

- Revelation 21:27; 22:15

Negative: don't tell lies
Positive: speak the truth
Reason: we are members of one body

Lying is a relationship killer since we can no longer know or trust the person we are trying to relate to. Relationships are built on trust, and trust is built on knowing the person. Deception undermines both knowledge and trust. Instead of lying, we are to speak the truth. We should be honest, real, and genuine with each other because we are members of the same body. The eyes must tell the rest of the body when it's okay to cross the busy street. If the eyes lie to the other members, the whole body will suffer (eyes included). We tell the truth because we are all connected in Christ.

> Positive: you can be angry
> Negative: do not act out your anger sinfully
> Negative: do not harbor anger
> Negative/Reason: do not give Satan a foothold

Although some want to translate the first part of 4:26 as a condition ("if you get angry"), it is a positive command with no evidence of a condition. It probably does not mean, however, that Christians are required to get angry on a regular basis, but only that they may get angry at certain times. Anger is not sinful in itself since this term is used for God's anger many times (e.g., Exod. 22:24; Judg. 2:14; 2 Chron. 29:8; Ps. 2:12). Jesus got angry enough to condemn the temple (Matt. 21). When God gets angry, however, he is in control of his anger while we often allow our anger to control us. Like gasoline, anger must be used properly (internal combustion) or it will explode.

The positive command is followed by three negative commands that modify the use of anger. If the "sunset limit" is not observed, we are asking for trouble. Like an aggressive cancer, anger can quickly grow into resentment and bitterness. By nurturing anger, we are giving the devil a "foothold" (a "place" or "opportunity"). Anger must be dealt with quickly or Satan will use it to damage both the individual Christian and the body of Christ. The devil doesn't cause anger, but he often exploits it to destroy relationships.

> Negative: stop stealing
> Positive: work hard
> Reason: so that you will be able to share

Instead of stealing, we are commanded to work hard. The word for "work" in 4:28 suggests working hard to the point of weariness (Luke 5:5; Acts 20:35; Rom. 16:6, 12; 1 Cor. 4:12; Col. 1:29; 1 Thess. 5:12; 1 Tim. 5:17). We don't work merely to accumulate wealth or indulge ourselves. Rather, we work diligently so that we will have enough to share with other believers in their time of need. When we stop stealing and start working, we are able to give to our community instead of draining it (terms like "mooch" or "sponge" come to mind).

What image does the word "unwholesome" bring to mind in these two contexts?

- Matthew 7:17–18; 12:33; Luke 6:43

- Matthew 13:48

When our words are beneficial and edifying, we actually contribute to the spiritual growth of other believers. We become avenues of God's grace. With our words we either build up or tear down. We don't want to give the devil a place and we don't want to make the Holy Spirit feel out of place. Critical, slanderous, divisive words against other members of the body upset the Holy Spirit, the very one who has stamped us with his character and promised to protect us until the day he redeems us.

> Negative: no unwholesome talk
> Positive: only beneficial, edifying talk
> Reason: so that your talk will give grace to others
> Negative/Reason: do not grieve the Holy Spirit

Paul concludes this section on walking in holiness by giving a short list of vices to be removed (largely focused on anger) and virtues to be embraced (focused on love). We should abandon every kind of bitterness or resentment, anger (rage) and wrath (hostility), quarreling (screaming or shouting), and abusive speech. Instead, God calls us to be kind, compassionate, and forgiving. The words for "forgiving" and "forgave" relate to the idea of showing favor or being gracious. We are gracious to others because God has been gracious to us in Christ. Rather than destroying others, we extend grace to them because we have been given grace by God. As it says in 1 John 4:19, "We love because he first loved us." If we refuse to give grace, we destroy the bridge over which we too must pass.

> Negative: don't be bitter or malicious
> Positive: be compassionate and forgiving
> Reason: God has forgiven you in Christ

So What?

1. Why would people who have already put off the old and put on the new need a list of practical instructions on how to live?

2. Why are we tempted to resort to lies? Similarly, why do we sometimes find it difficult to tell the truth? Perhaps those who have learned the hard way about the destructive power of lying will have some wisdom to share with the rest of the group. Any volunteers?

3. Snodgrass writes, "Anger is a means of communicating what we care about—usually ourselves—and is an attempt at punishment. It is a chemical and physiological reaction to our displeasure that the world is not as we wish."[31] How do we know when we are using anger in righteous ways or when we are giving the devil a foothold?

---

[31] Snodgrass, *Ephesians*, 257.

4. Are there ways that believers today can "steal" rather than work even though they might not be violating the law? Any suggestions that will help our friends become productive workers and givers?

5. We have all let unwholesome words escape our mouths. What are some small, specific steps we can take to move beyond such rotten talk to gracious, edifying speech?

6. If believers who claim to have experienced the grace of God do not feel his love and acceptance at the deepest levels, they will not extend grace to others. How can we help each other recognize and accept God's grace we have already been given in Christ?

15

NEW WALK IN LOVE

Ephesians 5:1-6

¹ Follow God's example, therefore, as dearly loved children ² and walk in the way of love, just as Christ loved us and gave himself up for us as a fragrant offering and sacrifice to God. ³ But among you there must not be even a hint of sexual immorality, or of any kind of impurity, or of greed, because these are improper for God's holy people. ⁴ Nor should there be obscenity, foolish talk or coarse joking, which are out of place, but rather thanksgiving. ⁵ For of this you can be sure: No immoral, impure or greedy person—such a person is an idolater—has any inheritance in the kingdom of Christ and of God. ⁶ Let no one deceive you with empty words, for because of such things God's wrath comes on those who are disobedient.

For the third time in Ephesians, Paul talks about how Christians should "walk" or live (4:1, 17; 5:2). Along with walking in unity (4:1-16) and holiness (4:17-32), we should also walk in love (5:1-6). Walking in love has a positive side (vv. 1-2) as well as a negative side (vv. 3-6). Loving God means that we walk toward him and with him and walk away from competing gods and idols. Walking in love means not only saying "yes" to God, but also saying "no" to evil.

The word "therefore" (v. 1) reminds us that we are still applying the deep truths and realities that were proclaimed in the first three chapters of the book. Our walk or lifestyle is a response to all that God has done for us. We are to "follow God's example as dearly loved children." To imitate means to impersonate or copy. Look up the following passages on imitation and write down your thoughts about each one:

- 1 Corinthians 4:16

- 1 Corinthians 11:1

- Philippians 3:17

- 1 Thessalonians 1:6

- 1 Thessalonians 2:14

- 2 Thessalonians 3:7, 9

- Hebrews 6:12

In your opinion, what does it mean to imitate or follow God's example "as dearly loved children"? How does this phrase add to the command?

The command in verse 2 to walk in love explains more specifically what is involved in imitating God. Since "God is love" (1 John 4:8), becoming more like God means becoming more loving. This present-tense command suggests that we are to make a habit of loving. Throughout Ephesians we are challenged to love: 4:2, 15, 16; 5:2, 25, 28, 33; 6:4. Paul had prayed specifically in 3:14–19 that we would know the love of Christ (although our knowledge can never exhaust his love).

Do you have a good definition of biblical love that can help you know when you are "walking in love"?

Photo 15. *"Gordon's Calvary." The site outside Jerusalem where some believe Jesus was crucified. The cross reminds us that Christ's love was costly and sacrificial.*

Perhaps the second half of verse 2 can help us know what it means to love. One writer sums it up this way: "To imitate the Father, love like the Son."[32] Jesus "loved us and gave himself up for us" when he died on the cross for us (see Eph. 5:25; Rom. 8:32; Gal. 2:20). The word "gave" means to "hand over" or "deliver." There is a word play between pagans who "have given themselves over to sensuality so as to indulge in every kind of impurity" (4:19), and Jesus who voluntarily gave himself over to be crucified. His supreme sacrifice became a sweet-smelling offering to the Father that fulfilled all the sacrifices required in the Old Testament. He died in our place and for our sake as the ultimate expression of God's love.

Now Paul tells us that the very opposite of sacrificial love is selfish sensuality (5:3–6). Christians are to imitate the Father by loving like the Son, not by lusting like the world. How would you sum up the message of verses 3–6?

---

[32] Edwards, *Galatians, Ephesians, Philippians*, 182.

The phrase "among you" means among those who follow Jesus. Three particular vices are mentioned as inappropriate for Christ followers (cf. 4:19). The first vice listed is "sexual immorality" (*porneia*), a term that denotes "any kind of illegitimate sexual intercourse, especially adultery and sexual relations with prostitutes."[33] The second vice—"any kind of impurity"—is often used by Paul in connection with sexual sin. Notice how these two vices appear together in the following passages: 1 Thessalonians 4:3, 7; Galatians 5:19; 2 Corinthians 12:21; Colossians 3:5. The third vice is "greed." What do you think greed has to do with sexual sins?

A Good Gift

❝ The reason why Christians should dislike and avoid vulgarity is not because we have a warped view of sex, and are either ashamed or afraid of it, but because we have a high and holy view of it as being in its right place God's good gift, which we do not want to see cheapened. All God's gifts, including sex, are subjects for thanksgiving, rather than for joking. To joke about them is bound to degrade them; to thank God for them is the way to preserve their worth as the blessings of a loving Creator.[34] ❞

Greed is the desire for more, including desiring someone else's body for selfish gratification. Not only must God's people ("saints") not be involved in such sins, they should also avoid talking about them—they "must not even be named among you" (NASB). Lincoln says:

The assumption behind this prohibition is that thinking and talking about sexual sins creates an atmosphere in which they are tolerated and which can indirectly even promote their practice.[35]

---

[33] O'Brien, *Ephesians*, 359.

[34] Stott, *Ephesians*, 193.

[35] Lincoln, *Ephesians*, 322.

Along with inappropriate conduct (5:3), Paul adds inappropriate speech to his prohibitions. What are the three kinds of speech that Paul forbids in 5:4? How are they translated in the Bible translation you normally use?

_____ — _____

_____ — _____

_____ — _____

Like the three vices of verse 3, the three speech sins of verse 4 are inappropriate. God's people are "saints" or holy ones and that characterization simply doesn't fit with sexual immorality, sensual greed, shameful speech, foolish talk, or degrading humor. It would be like mixing delicious Blue Bell or Ben & Jerry's ice cream with raw sewage. Disgusting!

In strong contrast to the six vices of 5:3–4 stands "thanksgiving." Instead of doing and saying all this junk, we should be thankful to the Lord. Why do you think Paul would choose the virtue of thanksgiving as the opposite of these vices?

To challenge "new people" in Christ not to live like the "old people" they once were, Paul concludes with a stern warning that "no immoral, impure or greedy person—such a person is an idolater—has any inheritance in the kingdom of Christ and of God" (5:6). The three vices of verse 3 are mentioned again in verse 6. Paul is not speaking here of an authentic follower who occasionally falls into sin. Rather, he is referring to a person who is characterized by such things because of intentional, habitual, unrepentant behavior. Such a person has given himself up to a shameful, ungodly lifestyle. "Idolaters" put themselves or other people or other things in the center, where God alone deserves to be. The warning says that no such person *has* (present tense) any part in God's heavenly kingdom. Instead, these "disobedient" people can expect to receive "God's wrath"—his holy condemnation and judgment on sin. Believers sometimes need to be warned because a pagan environment can send powerful temptations our way (e.g., 1 Cor. 6:9–11; Gal. 5:21). Believers should not be misled or

deceived by false teachers who suggest that how we live makes no difference. It makes all the difference—both in this world and the next.

So What?

1. Sometimes knowing whether we are actually loving another person can be difficult. We get confused by our own feelings, by certain circumstances, by the other person's reactions, by advice from
friends, and so on. How does the nature of Christ's love for us help
us know how best to love others?

2. Do you see a strong connection between sexuality and a person's
relationship to God? Why or why not?

3. How could just talking about what is not appropriate cause someone to stumble?

4. When do wit, humor, and clever speech go too far and degenerate into ungodly speech?

5. Let's say that you want to be a grateful, thankful person, but you're finding it very difficult. What wisdom can your community group give you for becoming a person of gratitude?

6. When we feel hopeless and helpless even though we are trusting God, we need his comfort and assurance. When we are rebellious and unashamed, our cold hearts need his warning. You might share with each other where you are in your walk with the Lord and take time to pray for each other.

16

NEW WALK IN LIGHT

Ephesians 5:7-14

⁷ Therefore do not be partners with them. ⁸ For you were once darkness, but now you are light in the Lord. Live as children of light ⁹ (for the fruit of the light consists in all goodness, righteousness and truth) ¹⁰ and find out what pleases the Lord. ¹¹ Have nothing to do with the fruitless deeds of darkness, but rather expose them. ¹² It is shameful even to mention what the disobedient do in secret. ¹³ But everything exposed by the light becomes visible—and everything that is illuminated becomes a light. ¹⁴ This is why it is said: "Wake up, sleeper, rise from the dead, and Christ will shine on you."

The very first thing God created was physical light (Gen. 1:3–4). A short time later, however, spiritual darkness entered the picture (Gen. 3). Not until the very end of the story does God's light dispel all darkness completely: "There will be no more night. They will not need the light of a lamp or the light of the sun, for the Lord God will give them light" (Rev. 22:5). Between the beginning of light and the end of darkness, the image of light appears as an important biblical theme.

What are some characteristics of physical light?

The image of physical light helps us understand spiritual light. The symbol of light is used to describe the very character of God: "God is light; in him there is no darkness at all" (1 John 1:5). Paul tells us in 1 Timothy 6:16 that God "alone is immortal and . . . lives in unapproachable light, whom no one has seen or can see." Jesus Christ entered the world as the "light of the world" (John 1:4–5, 9; 8:12; 9:5; 12:46). Look up each passage below and write down your thoughts about how believers are called to live in the light.

Matthew 5:14–16

John 3:20–21

Romans 13:11–14

1 Corinthians 4:5

Colossians 1:12–13

Philippians 2:14–16

1 Peter 2:9

1 John 1:5–7

Connection between Physical and Spiritual Light

>> For God, who said, 'Let light shine out of darkness,' made his
light shine in our hearts to give us the light of the knowledge of
God's glory displayed in the face of Christ. (2 Cor. 4:6) >>

We have been challenged to walk in unity, in holiness, and in love. Now
we are called to walk in light. It shouldn't surprise you that this section
opens with a command: "do not be partners with them" (v. 7). The word
"partner" means to share with someone, either sharing a possession or
sharing in a relationship. The only other time the word is used is in Ephesians 3:6, where we are told that "through the gospel the Gentiles are heirs
together with Israel, members together of one body, and *sharers together*
in the promise in Christ Jesus." We are not to be partners with "them," referring to "those who are disobedient" mentioned in 5:6. In other words,
followers of Christ are not to partner with unbelievers in their sins. What
light does 2 Corinthians 6:14–7:1 shed on the whole idea of a Christian
partnering with darkness?

The reason for not partaking with unbelievers is given in verse 8: "you
were once darkness, but now you are light in the Lord." Darkness often
serves as a symbol of sin and evil. Light, on the other hand, represents
"goodness, righteousness [or right behavior], and truth" (v. 9). Paul doesn't
merely say that we are in the light or that we should move toward the light,
but that we are light. We *were once* darkness, but now we *are* light. To keep
us humble and dependent, we need to remember that we are light "in the
Lord." We are light only because we are in relationship with Jesus, not because we are morally superior in and of ourselves. Look at all of Ephesians
4:17–5:14 and identify some characteristics of light and darkness:

Light	Darkness

At conversion, we are transferred from the kingdom or sphere of darkness to the kingdom of light (Col. 1:13). We are light and we live in the kingdom of light because we belong to God who is light. Now Paul reminds us to "live as children of light . . . find out what pleases the Lord" (5:8b, 10). The word translated "find out" tells us how we are to live as children of light. This word means to "examine and evaluate issues in order to determine the right course of action."[36] The word is used in a similar way in Romans 12:2 (when our minds are renewed we may "test and approve" the good, pleasing, and perfect will of God) and Philippians 1:10 (in answer to prayer that our love may abound in knowledge and insight, we will be able to "discern" what is best). Walking as children of light means that we use our minds to discern what pleases the Lord. Christians can't turn off their brains and expect to please God. Being thoughtful, discerning, and wise is a part of walking in the light.

But Paul goes even farther. Instead of participating in the unfruitful deeds of darkness—secret deeds that are too shameful even to mention (5:12)—we are rather to "expose them" (5:11). This is not an easy text to understand. While a few commentators think this calls for believers to rebuke other believers who are participating in dark deeds (e.g., Hoehner), the context supports the majority of scholars who think the command calls for exposing the dark deeds of unbelievers. The question is how do we do this?

Verses 13–14 offer us clues about how to expose the "fruitless deeds of darkness." While verbal rebuke of unbelievers cannot be ruled out, there

---

[36] O'Brien, *Ephesians*, 369.

Photo 16. *Inside the small, dark Mamertine Prison in Rome, where Paul was likely held before his death. Ironically, although Paul could be imprisoned in this dark, damp hole, his message of light eventually broke out and changed not only Rome, but also the entire world.*

are two other ways that seem more profitable. First, we are told that "everything exposed by the light becomes visible—and everything that is illuminated becomes a light" (5:13). Believers are light and the presence of light has the power to expose and transform the darkness. As we refuse to participate in evil, but live a godly life instead, our light (beaming out from our relationship with Christ) will pierce the darkness and expose it for what it really is. In other words, the first way that Christians expose the darkness is by living as children of light and letting their lives bear the visible fruit of goodness, righteousness, and truth. Now we see why it is so damaging for Christians to embrace the same beliefs, values, and lifestyle as non-Christians.

A second way that believers can expose the darkness is by verbally sharing God's story with unbelievers so that they experience a conversion to Christ. Verse 14 is probably a part of an early Christian hymn or saying ("it is said") that was sung or read when a new convert was baptized: "Wake up, sleeper, rise from the dead, and Christ will shine on you" (5:14). Drawn from portions of the Old Testament (Isa. 26:19 and 60:1–2), this saying would have reminded new believers that while they were once spiritually asleep, dead, and shrouded in darkness, they are now awake, alive, and walking in the light of Jesus Christ. When believers share the story of Christ with unbelievers, some of them respond and decide to make it their story also. Darkness is turned into light. Night becomes day.

So What?

1. As you looked up verses and made observations related to light and darkness, how would you say this theme relates to your life right now?

2. What are some deeds of darkness that many believers you know are tempted to participate in?

3. How can believers separate from the sins of unbelievers without conveying a "holier-than-thou" attitude?

4. Part of walking in the light is to "find out what pleases the Lord."
   What helps you most to discern what pleases God on a daily basis?

5. Has anyone in your group had an experience that you can share of
   exposing darkness (either through unbelievers seeing a difference
   in your life or through your verbal witness to Christ)?

17

NEW WALK IN WISDOM (PART I)

Ephesians 5:15-21

¹⁵ Be very careful, then, how you live—not as unwise but as wise, ¹⁶ making the most of every opportunity, because the days are evil. ¹⁷ Therefore do not be foolish, but understand what the Lord's will is. ¹⁸ Do not get drunk on wine, which leads to debauchery. Instead, be filled with the Spirit, ¹⁹ speaking to one another with psalms, hymns, and songs from the Spirit. Sing and make music from your heart to the Lord, ²⁰ always giving thanks to God the Father for everything, in the name of our Lord Jesus Christ. ²¹ Submit to one another out of reverence for Christ.

We have learned how to walk in unity (4:1–16), in holiness (4:17–32), in love (5:1–6), and in light (5:7–14). Now we look at walking in wisdom (5:15–6:9). We definitely need wisdom to live as children of light and expose the darkness. Certainly Paul's words in 5:15 make sense: "be very careful, then, how you live." The word "careful" suggests accuracy and precision. We must pay very close attention to how we live. People are watching!

What does it mean to walk carefully? Paul answers that question using three contrasts, each with a "do not" (negative command) followed by a "do" (positive command):

15	*not* as unwise, *but* as wise
17	*not* as foolish, *but* with understanding
18	*not* getting drunk, *but* being filled by the Spirit

First, walking carefully means that we do not walk unwisely, but wisely. God's wisdom is connected to his master plan in Christ (1:8–9, 17–18; 3:10). That is reality. We are wise when we understand God's plan (the "mystery") and bring our lives into conformity with that plan. The "unwise" either do not understand or do not accept what God is doing in this world. Their decisions and ambitions are disconnected from God's will.

Believers, on the other hand, live wisely by "making the most of every opportunity" (v. 16). In Colossians 4:5 Paul says something very similar—"Be wise in the way you act toward outsiders; make the most of every opportunity." Life is short and living wisely means we use our time well and seize every opportunity to please the Lord. The opposite is, of course, wasting or squandering time. We ought to grab opportunities "because the days are evil." The present age is described as evil or fallen (e.g., Gal. 1:4; Eph. 6:13) and lies under the influence of the "ruler of the kingdom of the air" (Eph. 2:2–3). But as Harold Hoehner reminds us,

> he [Paul] is not recommending that they fear the present evil age or avoid interaction with it. Rather his exhortation is to walk wisely in the evil days by seizing every opportunity. Unrelenting warfare exists between the God of heaven and gods of this age. . . . believers are commanded not to let the god of this age intimidate them, but to take advantage of every opportunity in this immoral environment to live a life that pleases God.[37]

Our Hurried Society

We seem determined to pack as many activities into as brief a time as possible. We are too busy for life. . . . Most households in our society spend at least four or five hours a day watching TV, . . . other 'diversions' take our attention too. But how much time do we give to life with God or to learning about that life? How much is invested in people or in doing something beneficial? We must not fritter away our lives on unproductive diversions and learn instead to invest time in our faith.[38]

The second "not . . . but" contrast occurs in verse 17: "do not be foolish, but understand what the Lord's will is." Because of everything Paul has

---

[37] Hoehner, *Ephesians*, 695.
[38] Snodgrass, *Ephesians*, 308.

just said in verses 15–16 ("therefore"), he commands us not to be foolish. What comes to mind when you hear the word "fool" or "foolish"?

The opposite of foolishness is "understanding." God wants us to perceive and comprehend and know and live out his will. He has already made known his will (1:9) and he expects us to do his will from the heart (6:6). In Ephesians (as in much of the New Testament) "God's will" is much bigger than how individual Christians should make decisions about their future. Rather, God's will is first about God and his plans. Perhaps it is even foolish to neglect the "small things" that we know God wants us to do today or even this minute because we are focusing too much on the "big things" that God might want us to do next year. As it often turns out, the "small things" might be the "big things."

The third contrast is in verse 18: "Do not get drunk on wine, which leads to debauchery. Instead, be filled by the Spirit." This command does not prohibit the drinking of wine, but it does prohibit getting drunk. Of course, in a culture like ours where binge drinking, alcohol addiction, and drunk driving are major problems, one could make a good case for abstaining altogether. Drunkenness leads to "debauchery"—foolish, undisciplined, wasteful living (cf. Luke 15:13, where the prodigal son squanders his wealth with a "wild lifestyle"). An intoxicated person gives up control to a substance and forfeits the ability to discern and do the will of God.

In contrast to drunkenness, believers are to "be filled by the Spirit." What an amazing command. Look at the following characteristics of this command and then write out your own translation of verse 18b in the space below:

- Present tense—ongoing or repeated filling ("keep on . . .")
- Imperative mood—a command to be filled!
- Passive voice—the Spirit does the filling, but we must allow him to fill us
- Plural—not just for "super-Christians" or church leaders, but for all believers

Paul says in Ephesians 1:13–14 that at conversion a person hears the gospel, believes in Christ, is included in Christ, and is sealed with (or baptized with or indwelt by) the Holy Spirit. That is a one-time experience, not to be repeated in the life of a believer. Here in Ephesians 5:18, however, Paul speaks of our need to "keep on allowing ourselves to be filled by the Spirit"! This is synonymous with "walking by the Spirit" (Gal. 5). It's not that we get more of the Spirit, but that the Spirit gets more of us. How will you know if you are allowing the Spirit to fill you? Check out the results.

The consequences or results of being filled by the Spirit are spelled out in 5:19–21. Some translations obscure this connection by translating these terms as separate commands—speak, sing, make music, submit. But the action words in verses 19–21 are not stand-alone commands. Rather, they are all totally connected to the key action word—"be filled" in verse 18. In other words, when you are genuinely filled by the Spirit, you will naturally display certain attitudes and actions.

A Spirit-filled person will be a person of worship—"speaking to one another with psalms, hymns, and songs from the Spirit. Sing and make music from your heart to the Lord . . ." Worship often involves singing (psalms, hymns, songs from the Spirit, make music) and there are two aspects of music in worship: we encourage, edify, and instruct "one another" with our singing, and we also praise "the Lord." Our praise and adoration should be "from our hearts," meaning with our whole being (and not just with our minds or our emotions).

A Spirit-filled person will also be a person of gratitude—"always

Photo 17. *Papyrus Oxyrhynchus 1786 is the oldest known manuscript of an early Christian hymn to contain both musical notation and lyrics. It's our only surviving example of pre-Gregorian Christian music. Discovered in the Egyptian town by that name, the hymn dates to the early 3rd century AD and calls for creation to fall silent so that the Triune God may be praised by his people.*

Translation:

1   . . . together all the eminent ones of God . . .

2   . . . [night] nor day (?) Let it/them be silent. Let the luminous stars not [ ],

3   . . . [let the rushings of winds, the sources] of all surging rivers [cease]. While we hymn

4   Father and Son and Holy Spirit, let all the powers answer, "Amen, amen, Strength, praise,

5   [and glory forever to God], the sole giver of all good things. Amen, amen."*]

*   Cosgrove, *Ancient Christian Hymn*, 37.

giving thanks to God the Father for everything, in the name of our Lord Jesus Christ, ..." When we acknowledge God and his good purposes for our lives, we give thanks. People who receive grace respond with thanksgiving.

A Spirit-filled person will also be a person of submission—"Submit to one another out of reverence [fear] for Christ." Because of our deep fear and awe of the Lord, we respect, defer, and yield to one another. Only the Spirit of God can create in us a humble, sacrificial love for one another.

SO WHAT?

1. What are some common ways that we waste and squander the precious gift of time and fail to "take advantage of every opportunity"? How do workaholics also fail in this area?

2. Can you think of a good example or illustration of "foolish" vs. "understanding" when it comes to how believers live, especially in relation to unbelievers?

3. How exactly do we allow the Spirit to fill us? What are we supposed to do?

4. What seems to be the main point of these three "not ... but ..." contrasts? How would you sum up in one sentence Paul's advice about walking wisely?

5. Why do you suppose Paul (under the inspiration of the Spirit) chose worship, gratitude, and submission as distinguishing marks of a Spirit-filled person?

6. How does this passage help us to know when our worship is authentic and genuine (as opposed to deceiving ourselves and others)?

18

New Walk in Wisdom (Part 2)

Ephesians 5:21-33

²¹ Submit to one another out of reverence for Christ. ²² Wives, submit yourselves to your own husbands as you do to the Lord. ²³ For the husband is the head of the wife as Christ is the head of the church, his body, of which he is the Savior. ²⁴ Now as the church submits to Christ, so also wives should submit to their husbands in everything. ²⁵ Husbands, love your wives, just as Christ loved the church and gave himself up for her ²⁶ to make her holy, cleansing her by the washing with water through the word, ²⁷ and to present her to himself as a radiant church, without stain or wrinkle or any other blemish, but holy and blameless. ²⁸ In this same way, husbands ought to love their wives as their own bodies. He who loves his wife loves himself. ²⁹ After all, no one ever hated their own body, but they feed and care for their body, just as Christ does the church—³⁰ for we are members of his body. ³¹ "For this reason a man will leave his father and mother and be united to his wife, and the two will become one flesh." ³² This is a profound mystery—but I am talking about Christ and the church. ³³ However, each one of you also must love his wife as he loves himself, and the wife must respect her husband.

The final result of being filled with the Spirit is "submitting to one another out of reverence for Christ" (v. 21). Along with worship and gratitude, submission is a distinguishing characteristic of people who are full of God's Spirit. Because of our reverence for the Lord, we yield to one another. Often the greatest challenge to submitting to one another comes at home. Howard Hendricks, long-time professor at Dallas Seminary, once said, "If your Christianity doesn't work at home, it doesn't work." There is a character in John Bunyan's classic *Pilgrim's Progress* who is said to be "a saint abroad, and a devil at home." These are hard sayings, but who we are at home, with our friends and family—those who know us best, is indeed who we really are. Only the Spirit of God can work a deep change in our hearts so that our most fundamental relationships display submission and love. In 5:22–33 Paul speaks to wives and husbands about their roles within the Christian household.

Regrettably, many translations separate verses 21 and 22 and sever the vital link between being filled by the Spirit (5:15–21) and following Christ in our family relationships (5:22–6:9). Verse 21 is a bridge verse, connecting these two important sections (5:15–21 and 5:22–33). In fact, the Greek text of verse 22 doesn't contain the verb "submit." It simply reads, "wives to your own husbands as to the Lord." The verb "submit" in verse 22 is implied from verse 21, where all Christians are called to submit to one another. Again, there is a crucial connection between our relationship with God and our relationships at home. The two should not be separated.

Wives are clearly commanded to submit to their husbands. The command is "submit yourselves," implying that the wife is free and responsible for carrying out this command voluntarily. This is not something the husband can force her to do. Paul does not tell wives to "obey" their husbands as he later instructs children to obey their parents. Neither does the Bible teach that wives are somehow inferior to their husbands. Paul affirms in Galatians 3:28 the equality, value, and dignity of all people in Christ—"There is neither Jew nor Gentile, neither slave nor free, nor is there male and female—for you are all one in Christ Jesus." Being equal, however, does not make wives and husbands identical. There is a difference in responsibility and role. We know what it is like to follow the lead of a church pastor, but no one believes that he or she is inferior to that church leader. Paul is teaching an "ordered equality" and we suffer when we ignore either aspect. God has established certain authority roles within the family and "submission is a humble recognition of that divine ordering."[39]

> ### "Submit/Submission" in Paul's Letters
>
> A sinful mind does not submit to God's law—Rom. 8:7
>
> Unbelievers did not submit to God's righteousness—Rom. 10:3
>
> Creation subjected to frustration—Rom. 8:20
>
> Refusing to submit to legalism—Gal. 2:5
>
> Submit to governing authorities—Rom. 13:1, 5; Titus 3:1
>
> Spirit of prophets submits to the prophets—1 Cor. 14:32
>
> Women must be in submission in worship—1 Cor. 14:34; 1 Tim. 2:11
>
> All creation submits to Christ—1 Cor. 15:27, 28; Eph. 1:22; Phil. 3:21
>
> Christ submits to the Father—1 Cor. 15:28
>
> All believers are to submit to other believers—1 Cor. 16:16; Eph. 5:21
>
> Believers submit to God—2 Cor. 9:13
>
> Church submits to Christ—Eph. 5:24
>
> Wives submit to husbands—Eph. 5:22, 24; Col. 3:18; Titus 2:5
>
> Children submit to parents—1 Tim. 3:4
>
> Slaves submit to masters—Titus 2:9

---

[39] O'Brien, *Ephesians*, 411.

The word "submit" suggests a subordination or yielding on the part of the one who is under the authority of another. Notice how Paul uses the word elsewhere in his writings. For instance, during the incarnation, Christ is subordinate to the Father. In 5:33 when Paul summarizes his teaching on the husband-wife relationship, he uses the word "respect" as a synonym for submission.

Notice too that wives are to submit to "your own husbands" (as opposed to men in general) and they are to submit to their husbands "as you do to the Lord," providing the motive for submission. Christian wives should see devotion to their husbands as part of their devotion to Jesus Christ. A Christian wife cannot serve her Lord without submitting to her husband. The two are connected.

The reason that a wife should submit is "because the husband is the head of the wife." The term "head" expresses the idea of "rule" or "authority" (see 1 Cor. 11:3; Eph. 1:22; 4:15; Col. 1:18; 2:10). The headship or leadership of the husband is compared to Christ's headship over his body, the church. As the head of the church, Christ is also "the savior of the body"—a characteristic that is not shared by the husband (the word "now" that begins v. 24 is actually a very strong word of contrast). Nevertheless, "as the church submits to Christ, so also wives should submit to their husbands in everything." The phrase "in everything" suggests every area of life, meaning that a wife's relationship to her husband cannot be pushed aside as only a part of her total life with God. Also, the wife's submission is not based on whether or not the husband loves her like he should. No such condition is mentioned. Of course, this command is not without qualification and a wife should never submit to her husband when it involves clear disobedience to God (cf. Acts 5:29).

Paul now turns his attention to the responsibilities of husbands. His command that husbands love their wives is radical when compared to the prevailing custom of that day giving men unlimited power as head of the household. We expect Paul to tell the husbands not to rule over their wives too harshly or to be nice to their wives, advice that would have been acceptable in Roman society. But Paul goes far beyond what the culture approved to what God expected— "husbands love your wives *just as* Christ loved the church and gave himself for her" (v. 25).

Husbands are called to sacrificial love and the standard is not simply other husbands, but Christ himself. Christ's love was demonstrated supremely when he died on the cross for his bride, the church (i.e., "gave himself up for her"). Husbands are to love their wives with a willing-to-die kind of love. This present-tense command challenges husbands to keep on unconditionally and sacrificially loving their wives. There is no hint that the husband's love is only given if and when the wife submits.

The Privilege of Pouring Out

❝ If 'headship' means 'power' in any sense, then it is power to care, not to crush, power to serve, not to dominate, power to facilitate self-fulfillment, not to frustrate or destroy it. And in all this the standard of the husband's love is to be the cross of Christ, on which he surrendered himself even to death in his selfless love for his bride.[40] ❞

As you look at 5:25–32, what can you find in this section about how Christ loved the church?

In the same way that Christ loved his body, the church, so husbands ought to love their wives as their own bodies. Paul is probably applying the second great commandment ("You shall love your neighbor as yourself" in Lev. 19:18) directly to the husband-wife relationship. For the husband, the wife is his nearest neighbor and one worthy of sacrificial love. Even more, when the husband loves his wife, he also loves himself since the two of them are actually "one flesh" (v. 31 and Gen. 2:24). Healthy people don't hate their own bodies. Rather, they feed and care for their bodies. Christ not only "loved" the church (referring to the cross in the past), but he also "loves" the church (referring to his ongoing care for his people).

After he quotes Genesis 2:24 in verse 31 about the two becoming one flesh, Paul adds that "this is a profound mystery." God's design for marriage is profound and significant, especially as it reflects the relationship between Christ and his own bride, the church. The submission, respect, leadership, sacrificial love, and service within a Christian marriage actually mirrors Christ's love for his church and our own humble submission to his leadership.

---

[40] Stott, *Ephesians*, 232.

Paul finishes his teaching on this topic by reminding each husband to love his own wife as himself and each wife to respect her own husband. Love and respect—the two most important words for a successful Christian marriage.[41]

So What?

1. The command for a wife to submit to her husband is not politically correct in our culture, but it is very biblical. What does submission look like? What does it involve? (It will be easy to move quickly into a discussion of what it does *not* involve, but try to focus on what it might involve.)

2. How does the comparison of a wife's submission to her husband with the church's submission to Christ help us understand the role of a Christian wife?

3. How does Christ's love for the church help us to understand how husbands ought to treat their wives?

---

[41] A book that emphasizes both of these important truths is Eggerichs, *Love & Respect*.

4. What do think about Klyne Snodgrass's observation that "for those who are married, it [marriage] is the primary relationship for discipleship"?[42]

5. Do you know of a married couple where the qualities of love and respect are faithfully demonstrated? If so, what can you share about what you have observed that will help the group grasp the deep truths of this passage?

6. We sometimes forget that Christ is head of the church as we get bogged down in local church business, politics, or ministry. Since we are all in the role of "bride" when it comes to our relationship to Christ, what are some ways your local church can be more submissive to Christ?

---

[42] Snodgrass, *Ephesians*, 313.

19

New Walk in Wisdom (Part 3)

Ephesians 6:1-4

[1] Children, obey your parents in the Lord, for this is right. [2] "Honor your father and mother"—which is the first commandment with a promise—[3] "so that it may go well with you and that you may enjoy long life on the earth." [4] Fathers, do not exasperate your children; instead, bring them up in the training and instruction of the Lord.

Paul's teaching on relationships between parents and children in Ephesians occurs within the larger context of 5:19–6:9. When people are truly filled with God's Spirit, they worship wholeheartedly (5:19), they give thanks (5:20), and they yield or submit to one other (5:21). Our submission within the body of Christ cannot be restricted to adult relationships. The Holy Spirit is keenly interested in how parents and children get along and only he can give us the love and patience we need for healthy, holy relationships.

Before we look more closely at these four verses in Ephesians, look up each of the following references that deal with children or parents and see what they have to say. (These are only a few of the many Bible verses dealing with this topic).

- Psalm 127:3

- Proverbs 23:13–14; Hebrews 12:7–8

- Proverbs 20:11

- Proverbs 22:6

- Deuteronomy 4:9; 6:6–7

- Colossians 3:20–21

- Matthew 18:2–6

- Mark 10:13–16

- Matthew 11:25; Luke 10:21

- Matthew 7:9–11

- 1 Timothy 3:4–5

- 1 Timothy 5:4

Here in 6:1–4 Paul talks to both children and parents. When Paul mentions "children" he isn't talking about infants or even toddlers. In the original setting, the children would have been responsible members of the local church as it gathered in various households for worship, teaching, and fellowship. These kids had to be old enough to understand most of Paul's letter as it was read in that gathering and to exercise their freedom to do (or refuse to do) what he said. On the other hand, they had to be young enough to still be in the process of being brought up "in the training and instruction of the Lord" (v. 4). In general terms, these "children" probably ranged in age from 4–5 years up to the early or middle teens.

The word "parents" is mentioned in verse 1, "father and mother" in verse 2, and "fathers" in verse 4. While children should obey and honor both parents and both parents are to be involved in all bringing up the children, fathers are singled out as especially responsible.

Children are instructed in 6:1 to "obey" their parents "in the Lord." This doesn't mean that children are only supposed to obey Christian parents, but that children are to obey their parents as part of their own commitment to the Lord (cf. "as to the Lord" in 5:22; 6:6). In Colossians 3:20 Paul says practically the same thing in a different way: "Children, obey your parents in everything, for this pleases the Lord."

Photo 18. *At the site of the ancient church of Philadelphia, children greet a member of our study group with flowers.*

Surely all of us have childhood memories of asking our parents for things only to have them say "no." Children everywhere know to ask the natural follow-up question: "Why?" And we've all experienced the standard parental answer: "Because!" End of story.

Little did we know that parents got their response from the Bible. The motivation Paul gives for children to obey their parents is because "this is right." Children should obey their parents because it is the appropriate and fitting and proper thing to do in the eyes of the Lord. It's the right thing to do. "Because!"

In 6:2–3 Paul supports his instruction with quotations from the Old Testament (see below). As children grow up and leave the home, obedience is no longer an obligation. Honor, however, remains a lifetime calling (Matt. 15:4; 19:19; Mark 7:10; 10:19; Luke 18:20). The focus of this particular text is on younger children and "honor" and "obedience" are emphasizing the same thing. To obey our parents is to honor them and to disobey them is to dishonor them.

Exodus 20:12	Deuteronomy 5:16
Honor your father and your mother, that you may live long in the land the LORD your God is giving to you.	Honor your father and your mother, as the LORD your God has commanded you, so that you may live long and that it may go well with you in the land the LORD your God is giving you.

Paul says this is "the first commandment with a promise" (v. 2). The second of the ten commandments does carry a general promise (applicable to all the commandments) of punishment for those who reject God and faithfulness to those who obey him (Exod. 20:4–6). The fifth commandment about honoring our parents is the first one with a very specific promise connected only to this commandment. In Exodus and Deuteronomy, people who honor their parents are promised long life "in the land." Unlike the ancient Israelites, however, Christians don't have their hope set on life in the earthly "promised land." Does this mean that we should spiritualize the promise to refer to life in heaven? Most New Testament scholars don't think so. The promise is for well-being and long life on this earth. There will be exceptions to this general rule, but the rule still holds true: "obedience and honor foster self-discipline, which in turn brings stability, longevity, and well-being."[43] When kids listen to the advice of their parents and learn from the experience of their parents, they tend to live longer and better. That's the main point.

A Ministry Priority

In his book Transforming Children into Spiritual Champions, sociologist George Barna suggests that 'if people do not embrace Jesus Christ as Savior before they reach their teenage years, the chance of their doing so at all is slim.' He says that 'your spiritual condition by the age of 13 is a strong predictor of your spiritual profile as an adult.' 'More often than not,' Barna finds, 'what a person decides about truth, sin, forgiveness and eternal consequences during the preteen years is the same perspective that person carries to the

---

[43] Hoehner, *Ephesians*, 792.

grave.' Sadly, his research indicates that while 93 percent 'consider themselves to be Christian by age 13' . . . 'only 4 percent of all 13-year olds are classified as evangelicals [those with a biblical world-view that influences decision making].' Barna concludes: 'I am now convinced that the greatest hope for the local church lies in raising godly children.' We do this not by trying to 'get kids saved' before forgetting about them, but by helping them develop and live out a biblical worldview (in other words grow as a disciple of Jesus).[44] 🙶

Now Paul turns his attention to the responsibilities of the parents, specifically the task of the fathers. In the ancient world fathers had absolute authority over the children. They could punish them harshly, shame them publicly, sell them into slavery, and even kill them. But Paul doesn't mention any of these legal or cultural rights. Rather, he talks to fathers about how to allow the Lord to use them to shape their children. Radical advice!

First, fathers are told not to "exasperate your children," which means to provoke them to anger (cf. Rom. 10:19; Eph. 4:26). There are several ways that a father (or parent) can provoke a child to anger: (1) when we criticize or humiliate our kids, especially in public, (2) when we neglect or ignore them, (3) when we constantly condemn or belittle them, (4) when we are unreasonable and abuse our own authority by trying to control everything, (5) when we expect them to achieve beyond their ability, (6) when we are arbitrary, are inconsistent, and lack discipline ourselves. In the parallel passage in Colossians, Paul says that provoking our children causes them to lose heart or become discouraged (Col. 3:21). Children are people too! Someone once said that raising a child is like holding a wet bar of soap—you have to hold it firmly enough so that it won't slide out of your hand, but not so tightly that it shoots out of your hand. Firm, but gentle.

Second, fathers are instructed to "bring them up in the training and instruction of the Lord." Instead of causing them to rebel out of anger or lose heart out of frustration, parents are called to nurture their kids. The word "bring up" is used in Ephesians 5:29 to describe how a man "feeds" or nourishes his own body. Our job as parents is not crush our kids, but to care for them and cause them to flourish.

The expression "training and instruction of the Lord" tells us more about the atmosphere and context for raising our kids. The first word "training" refers to instructive discipline. The word is used in 2 Timothy

---

[44] Barna, *Transforming Children*, 34, 41, 46, 33, 49, respectively.

3:16 to refer to the "training in righteousness" that God's Word provides for all of us. The second word "instruction" includes counsel that involves correction and even warning. Surely parents are called not only to teach kids the right way to live, but also to steer them away from harmful and destructive paths. The phrase "of the Lord" probably qualifies both words and reminds us that we are not just teaching kids how to build fires or clean up rooms or ride bikes. Our instruction and discipline should be Christ-centered. We are called to raise up our kids in the ways of the Lord, not just the ways of human beings or the ways of the world.

So What?

1. What is involved specifically for a child to obey and honor his or her parents (e.g., actions such as listening, attitudes, etc.)?

2. Is the command to "obey your parents" an absolute command (i.e., to be obeyed under any circumstances)? If not, when should children disobey their parents?

3. Should the promise of a longer life be our primary motivation for honoring our parents? Why or why not?

4. What are some other actions, attitudes, and words—besides those listed above—that provoke a child to anger?

5. What are some specific things parents (especially fathers) can do to "train and instruct" their kids in the ways of the Lord? If you are an adult, what do you wish your parents had done more for you? If your kids are a bit older, what do you wish you had done more when they were younger?

6. Parents face many competing influences upon the lives of their children (e.g., music, movies, Internet, TV, magazines, friends). The primary responsibility for raising children lies with the parents, not with the church, but what are some specific ways the church can support parents?

20

New Walk in Wisdom (Part 4)

Ephesians 6:5-9

⁵ Slaves, obey your earthly masters with respect and fear, and with sincerity of heart, just as you would obey Christ. ⁶ Obey them not only to win their favor when their eye is on you, but as slaves of Christ, doing the will of God from your heart. ⁷ Serve wholeheartedly, as if you were serving the Lord, not people, ⁸ because you know that the Lord will reward each one for whatever good they do, whether they are slave or free. ⁹ And masters, treat your slaves in the same way. Do not threaten them, since you know that he who is both their Master and yours is in heaven, and there is no favoritism with him.

The way a Christian household works depends largely on how we live out Ephesians 5:21: "submit to one another out of reverence for Christ." And living out Ephesians 5:21 depends on how we obey the command in Ephesians 5:18 to "be filled by the Spirit." When we give ourselves to the Holy Spirit, he changes our relationships, even relationships between slaves and masters.

When we hear the word "slave," we tend to think of slavery that existed in the United States in the 1800s or some other modern form of slavery. But ancient Greco-Roman slavery was different from modern slavery.[45] Ancient slavery wasn't related to race or skin color at all. Sometimes free people who were poor or destitute actually sold themselves into slavery in order to receive the food, clothing, shelter, and medical care given to slaves. Others became slaves in order to climb in social standing. Slaves were often highly educated and worked in specialized professions such as property management, accounting, teaching, and medicine. They were allowed to save money and own property (even other slaves) and many eventually gained their freedom and became Roman citizens. The treatment of slaves varied widely and depended mostly on the masters. While some slaves were treated cruelly, others were well-treated and had more

---

[45] See Hoehner, *Ephesians*, 800–804.

of a family relationship with their masters. Since as many as one-third of the people in the Roman Empire were slaves, most churches certainly included both slaves and free persons. Paul's teaching here in 6:5–9 calls for the gospel of Christ to transform a person and his or her relationships. This change would lead to the transformation of society.

Take a second and look closely at the passage above. Make a list of every occurrence of "God" or "Christ" or "the Lord."

Why is it significant that Paul reasons and thinks theologically (in God-centered ways) here?

Changing Society

" For the early church to advocate revolt [against the institution of slavery] would have been the death of the Christian movement. Slavery and other social issues were not their focus; the gospel and its description of life were. . . . But as they presented life in Christ, they put in motion a process that would eventually destroy slavery. . . . Like Paul, we must find ways to say, 'The slave is your brother,' so that the system is subverted by the way people are valued and nurtured. Churches should lead the way in such thinking.[46] "

---

[46] Snodgrass, *Ephesians*, 328.

What is striking and rare is that Paul addresses the slaves directly. Normally the focus was put on how the masters were supposed to rule over their slaves. But here slaves are treated as valuable, responsible human beings who are full members of the Christian church. Paul's one command to slaves is to "obey your earthly masters." He spends most of his time explaining the heart attitudes and motives that should accompany this outward obedience. After each brief explanation below, write in your own words what you think Paul is trying to communicate:

- "with respect and fear"—an attitude of reverence (see also 1 Cor. 2:3; 2 Cor. 7:15; Phil. 2:12)

- "with sincerity of heart, just as you would obey Christ"—with a whole heart that is completely united in one purpose (singleness of heart or integrity), directed ultimately to Christ

- "not only to win their favor when their eye is on you"—avoid serving only to impress others or serving diligently only when others are watching

- "but as slaves of Christ, doing the will of God from your heart"— Christ is the ultimate audience and proper service to Christ (the will of God) begins with a heart devoted to him

- "Serve wholeheartedly, as if you were serving the Lord, not people"—serving a master with goodwill or enthusiasm (rather than ill-will), as though serving the Lord himself

Christian slaves should obey their earthly masters with an attitude of respect, sincerity, diligence, and goodwill or enthusiasm. Why? The reason is given in verse 8: "because you know that the Lord will reward each one for whatever good they do, whether they are slave or free." No doubt, many slaves had served faithfully without ever being noticed or rewarded by their masters. (Some of you know what it feels like to dedicate yourself totally to a cause or an organization without receiving the appropriate recognition.) Paul's words in verse 8 are extremely encouraging. Those servants don't need to worry about God also forgetting about them. He notices the good deeds of "each one." While earthly masters often fail to notice or reward, God never does. Although there is no promise here of an immediate reward, the faithful Christian servant will receive a reward on the day when the Lord will evaluate everyone according to their deeds (Rom. 2:6; 1 Cor. 3:10–15; 2 Cor. 5:10). The Lord himself will reward each slave individually for the good she or he has done. There is no need to maneuver for your master's attention or advertise your own accomplishments since your heavenly Master will recognize you properly on the last day.

God Does Not Play Favorites

God 'will repay each person according to what they have done.' To those who by persistence in doing good seek glory, honor and immortality, he will give eternal life. But for those who are self-seeking and who reject the truth and follow evil, there will be wrath and anger. There will be trouble and distress for every human being who does evil: first for the Jew, then for the Gentile; but glory, honor and peace for everyone who does good: first for

> the Jew, then for the Gentile. For God does not show favoritism.
> (Rom. 2:6–11) 〞

As with the other household relationships, Paul now speaks to the second party: the masters. What would be shocking for someone in that culture is to hear that slave owners must "treat your slaves the same way." This suggests that masters are to allow their relationship with the Lord to shape their attitudes and actions also. Instead of threatening, manipulating, humiliating, or abusing their servants, they should act with respect, integrity, sincerity, and goodwill. The Greek word *kyrios* is normally translated "Lord" but is also translated "master" in this context. This makes for a powerful and persuasive word play, especially for the masters. In other words, even these masters have a heavenly Master. The bosses have a Boss! Both the slaves and the masters are in fact slaves or servants of the Lord, since they have the same Master in heaven.

With the heavenly Master there is no favoritism or partiality. The word "favoritism" refers to someone making "unjust distinctions between people by treating one person better than another."[47] In all cultures, social status can lead to favoritism (e.g., preference is given to a famous person, a wealthy person gets special treatment, a beautiful person gains an unfair advantage). Paul is saying that God is not like this. As the Lord said to Samuel when he chose David as king: "The LORD does not look at the things people look at. People look at the outward appearance, but the LORD looks at the heart" (1 Sam. 16:7).

Snodgrass sums it up well:

> The message of this text obviously moves from ancient slavery to modern employer-employee relations, but it pushes us far beyond that. Its theology concerns who we really are, what motivates us, whom we seek to please, and how we use power. Every part of life is redefined.... Everything we do involves a direct encounter with Jesus Christ . . . no act is mundane and no person is unimportant. . . . And all of us stand on equal footing with the same Lord, who cares deeply how we treat each other and will hold us accountable.[48]

---

[47] Louw and Nida, *GELNT*, 88.238.

[48] Snodgrass, *Ephesians*, 328–29.

So What?

1. While the institution of slavery is not legal in our culture, do you see any social or economic structures today that continue to enslave people? If so, please explain.

2. Why do we sometimes fail to think theologically like Paul did (i.e., relate everything in life to God as the center of life)?

3. If you think about your own attitudes toward work or school in light of the attitudes described in verses 5–7, which ones do you need to work on the most?

4. What are some common situations where employees take advantage of generous employers? How should a Christian employer respond in light of this passage?

5. What are some common situations where employers mistreat employees? How should a Christian employee respond?

6. Overall, how does having one audience—the Lord—who does not play favorites and to whom you are accountable, help you be a better servant or boss?

21

New Walk in Strength

Ephesians 6:10–20

10 Finally, be strong in the Lord and in his mighty power. 11 Put on the full armor of God, so that you can take your stand against the devil's schemes. 12 For our struggle is not against flesh and blood, but against the rulers, against the authorities, against the powers of this dark world and against the spiritual forces of evil in the heavenly realms. 13 Therefore put on the full armor of God, so that when the day of evil comes, you may be able to stand your ground, and after you have done everything, to stand. 14 Stand firm then, with the belt of truth buckled around your waist, with the breastplate of righteousness in place, 15 and with your feet fitted with the readiness that comes from the gospel of peace. 16 In addition to all this, take up the shield of faith, with which you can extinguish all the flaming arrows of the evil one. 17 Take the helmet of salvation and the sword of the Spirit, which is the word of God. 18 And pray in the Spirit on all occasions with all kinds of prayers and requests. With this in mind, be alert and always keep on praying for all the Lord's people. 19 Pray also for me, that whenever I speak, words may be given me so that I will fearlessly make known the mystery of the gospel, 20 for which I am an ambassador in chains. Pray that I may declare it fearlessly, as I should.

Part of our new walk in Christ (in addition to walking in unity, holiness, love, light, and wisdom) includes walking in strength. Following Jesus often feels a lot more like a battleground than a playground. Life is tough enough by itself, but we also have supernatural enemies. Somewhat surprisingly, however, the emphasis here is not on attacking, but on resisting and standing firm (vv. 11, 13, 14). Christ has already won the victory over the powers of evil so we no longer need to live in fear or despair. Yet while the victory has been secured, we will still face attacks. Our task is to resist and hold our ground. And even then we are not standing in our own strength. It is the "armor of God" that we put on. We stand in the Lord's strength. This passage has three main parts:

6:10–13	be strong in the Lord so that we can stand
6:14–17	stand firm by taking up the armor of God
6:18–20	pray and stay alert as we fulfill our mission

The commands in this section include "be strong" (v. 10), "put on" (vv. 11, 13), "stand" (v. 14), and "take" (v. 17). In other words, we are to allow God to strengthen us, to make use of the protection he has provided (the armor), and to exercise our will in resisting the devil. We carry out these commands together as a community.

> " Mention of the 'schemes' of the devil reminds us of the trickery and subterfuge by which evil and temptation present themselves in our lives. Evil rarely looks evil until it accomplishes its goal; it gains entrance by appearing attractive, desirable, and perfectly legitimate. It is a baited and camouflaged trap."[49] "

Strength comes from the Lord, that is, from our relationship with the Lord. This power and strength are not just given by the Lord, they actually belong to the Lord. It is his very strength and might that we receive. In Ephesians 1:17–19 Paul had prayed that we might know the incomparable greatness of God's power available to us as demonstrated through the resurrection of Jesus Christ from the dead. Now, using the illustration of a Roman soldier in full battle attire, Paul tells us to make use of God's power by putting on the full armor of God. We need God's armor in order to stand against "the devil's schemes" and the other evil powers mentioned in verse 12. Our own "armor" is simply not strong enough.

Our struggle is not primarily with other human beings. Rather, it is a fight against unseen evil forces. These wicked forces mimic their dubious leader, the devil, by using lies and deceit and accusation as their weapons of choice. Satan's strategy hasn't changed. He wraps evil in a beautiful package and tries to sell it as good: "You deserve this" or "God is keeping this from you" or "This will make your life much better." Indeed, this scheme is a scam. Don't fall for it! If God gave us his only Son, it proves

---

[49] Snodgrass, *Ephesians*, 339.

beyond any doubt that he is not keeping anything from us. He wants only what is best for us.

To "stand" means to offer resistance or hold firmly to something. We're not told to attack the devil or to take the offensive. Instead, we are to play defense, to stand firm, to hold our ground. We are involved in a struggle to be sure, but our primary strategy is to hang on. We win the battle by enduring, by persevering, and by refusing to surrender to evil. Sometimes the best way to say "Yes" to God is to say "No" to evil. But since we are engaged in a real battle against the god of this world, we need God's armor in order to stand firm.

As we think about the armor of God, it is important to focus on the virtues and actions represented by the armor (e.g., truth, righteousness, and so on) rather than on the belt, sandals, shield, helmet, and sword. We shouldn't allow the analogy to become more important than the reality it illustrates. We stand firm by putting on the full suit of armor. The belt of truth likely represents both the truth that God has revealed in Jesus and the gospel (Eph. 1:13; 4:21). It also probably involves living out truth in our relationships (Eph. 4:15, 24–25; 5:9). Jesus prayed a very specific truth-based prayer for us in John 17:17: "Sanctify them by the truth; your word is truth." As we listen to the Lord by understanding and applying his word, we will be able to reject the lies of Satan and the world system and live in truth.

You're Not Alone!

> Be alert and of sober mind. Your enemy the devil prowls around like a roaring lion looking for someone to devour. Resist him, standing firm in the faith, because you know that the family of believers throughout the world is undergoing the same kind of sufferings. And the God of all grace, who called you to his eternal glory in Christ, after you have suffered a little while, will himself restore you and make you strong, firm and steadfast. To him be the power for ever and ever. Amen. (1 Peter 5:8–11)

The breastplate of righteousness probably refers not only to the righteousness of Christ that we are given at conversion, but also to righteous living. We are called to reflect God's righteous character in all our relationships (Eph. 4:24). This calls for discipline on our part since, as Leon Morris points out, you can slide into sin, but you cannot slide into righteousness.[50]

We also put on God's armor by fitting our feet with "readiness that comes from the gospel of peace" (v. 15). This preparation or readiness comes from the gospel of peace. This is not only about sharing the gospel (evangelism), but also about having a peaceful mind and heart ourselves (versus always being worried and fearful), as well as serving as an agent of peace. God desires that people be reconciled to one another in Christ (Eph. 2:11–22).

The shield of faith is especially important since it protects us from the "flaming arrows of the evil one" (Satan). The steadfast faith of a believer in community with other believers provides the necessary protection against the attacks of the devil, from "every kind of temptation to ungodly behavior, doubt, and despair, but also external assaults, such as persecution or false teaching."[51]

The last two pieces of armor include the helmet of salvation and the sword of the Spirit, which is the Word of God. The helmet is our experience of and assurance of God's salvation provided in Christ. We have been rescued

Photo 19. *Relief from Ephesus showing a soldier's armor*

from sin and Satan, and given new life in a new community. Relying on that reality protects us from the enemy. The sword is the only offensive weapon. The word used here (*rhēma*) is a synonym for the usual term for "word" (*logos*), with perhaps a bit more emphasis on the spoken nature of the word. In Matthew 4 when Jesus is tempted by the devil, he holds his ground by speaking God's Word in response ("it is written" in Matt. 4:4, 6, 7). The point here is not that we should shout random words of rebuke at the devil. The powers of darkness are not impressed by our emotional intensity. Rather, they tremble at God's truth. We follow Jesus' example by responding to spiritual attacks with God's Word. The Holy Spirit is the one who makes this "Word sword" sharp and effective (Heb. 4:12), but we must hold it and use it to fend off attacks.

The final section of this magnificent portion of Scripture deals with prayer and spiritual alertness. The analogy of the armor ends here as the mindset of the soldier comes into view. Notice all the words for prayer:

---

[50] Morris, *Reflections*, 200.

[51] O'Brien, *Ephesians*, 480.

pray, prayers, requests, and praying. We are supposed to pray "on all occasions," and remain "alert." The attack could come at any time. The powers of darkness are crafty and deceptive. We cannot stand in our strength alone. We need God's power and protection. We are on full alert as we carry out God's mission in this world. There is no time to let down our guard. We are called to "keep on praying," an idea calling us to "continue to do something with intense effort—to devote oneself to, to keep on, to persist in."[52]

We are called to pray for "all the Lord's people"—for the other members of the army. Spiritual warfare includes praying for our community. Paul began this letter by praying for his readers (Eph. 1:15–23). Now, he asks them to pray for him. Facing an upcoming trial before Caesar (likely Nero), Paul needs prayer in order to speak the "mystery of the gospel" (Jews and Gentiles being united in Christ) clearly and boldly. Instead of being respected as the ambassador or representative of Christ that he is, he finds himself in prison awaiting trial. Paul doesn't ask for money or safety or health or vindication. Instead, he asks his community to pray that he may speak boldly as he should when he is granted an audience with the emperor. Check out 2 Timothy 4:16–17 for God's answer.

SO WHAT?

1. How does it change your outlook to realize that we win by standing our ground and holding fast to what Christ has already accomplished, rather than by achieving a victory ourselves?

2. Have you ever thought of spiritual warfare mainly as holding your ground or standing firm? Talk about the defensive emphasis in warfare.

---

[52] Hoehner, *Ephesians*, 858–59.

3. Our struggle is "not against flesh and blood" and yet human beings are often seduced into participating with wicked powers in opposing Christ and his church. As believers, how do we stand against the powers of darkness without also hating and rejecting the human beings who have been deceived by them?

4. As you think about each piece of armor—truth, righteousness, gospel of peace, faith, salvation, the Word of God—which one(s) do you most need to put on right now in your life?

5. Can you think of times when you were attacked and would have fared much better had you been protected by a certain piece of armor? Care to explain?

6. What are some things that lull us into spiritual apathy and dull our spiritual awareness?

7. At the end of a long letter to close friends just before a trial before the most powerful person in the world who might condemn you to death, what would be your prayer requests?

22

CONCLUSION

Ephesians 6:21-24

²¹ Tychicus, the dear brother and faithful servant in the Lord, will tell you everything, so that you also may know how I am and what I am doing. ²² I am sending him to you for this very purpose, that you may know how we are, and that he may encourage you. ²³ Peace to the brothers and sisters, and love with faith from God the Father and the Lord Jesus Christ. ²⁴ Grace to all who love our Lord Jesus Christ with an undying love.

Who is your best friend? When you think of that person, don't you automatically think of your shared life experiences—the long conversations, the road trips, the times you laughed until you cried, the times you just cried, the times you trusted each other or asked for prayer or told them the good news? Friendships make life rich and meaningful and Ephesians has told us a lot about what it means to live in authentic community. As Paul closes this important letter, he mentions one of his best friends: Tychicus.

The New Testament mentions Tychicus five times: Acts 20:4; Ephesians 6:21; Colossians 4:7–8; 2 Timothy 4:12; Titus 3:12. We read in Acts that he was a native of Asia and since Ephesus was the leading city of Asia, Tychicus may have come to faith in Christ as a result of Paul's ministry in that region. He traveled with Paul on his third missionary journey. Most likely, the letters of Ephesians, Colossians and Philemon were all written about the same time and carried to their recipients by Tychicus (Col. 4:7–9). He probably accompanied Paul to Jerusalem when they took the collection from the Gentile churches to the needy Jewish believers in that city (Acts 20:4). Later, Paul sent Tychicus back to Ephesus on an important mission, perhaps to take over for Timothy (2 Tim. 4:12), and even thought about sending him to Crete to take Titus's place (Titus 3:12).

Here in 6:21–22, Paul refers to Tychicus as a "dear brother and faithful servant in the Lord," a description that speaks about how much he loved and trusted him. Tychicus and Paul had probably been through a lot. Tychicus may have listened to Paul teach for hours about Jesus. He may have seen Paul's bold and passionate public witness for Jesus. He may have watched the silversmiths lead the massive public riot against Paul's teachings about Christ in Ephesus (see Acts 19). Through it all, Tychicus had proven to be a faithful friend and a responsible co-worker.

Tychicus was just the kind of faithful servant Paul could trust with important work, such as bringing the letter to the Ephesian church and reporting on everything going on with Paul. In that day, there wasn't a reliable postal system for private letters, so they were carried by trusted friends traveling in the right direction. A close friend would supplement the letter with even more information about the letter writer and his circumstances. He might also provide more explanation of particular parts of the letter.

Paul assures the Ephesians that Tychicus is such a trusted friend and he will "tell you everything" so "that you may know how we are, and that he may encourage you." Since Paul was in prison, the Ephesian Christians needed some encouragement. Their "father in the faith" was suffering. When our leaders suffer, we tend to get discouraged and lose heart, and this seems to be happening in the Ephesian church as well (see 3:13). Paul reassured them that Tychicus would fill in the gaps and encourage them.

Paul the Letter Writer

“ When Paul decided to send a letter to Corinth, he contracted a secretary. It would have taken more than the usual haggling. A typical letter of that time was about the length of 3 John. Paul's letters were extraordinarily long. Paul's opponents ridiculed his letters as 'weighty' (2 Cor. 10:10). The secretary would bring a stack of wax tablets. In a typical scenario, as Paul speaks, the secretary scratches furiously on the tablets. Sosthenes interjects at times. Paul ponders and perhaps rephrases. Team members wander through the room at times, pausing to listen, offering suggestions. After several hours, the secretary leaves to prepare a rough draft of that portion. When the secretary returns a few days later, Paul listens to the draft, making corrections and additions. He then adds more to the letter. This process continues over the next few weeks until the letter is 100 percent precisely the way Paul wanted it, because as the primary sender, he is responsible for every word. The secretary brings the final draft to Paul (on nice papyrus and in good handwriting). As authentication (2 Thess. 3:17), Paul adds some closing remarks in his own handwriting, sometimes several verses (Gal. 6:11–18), sometimes just a line or two (1 Cor. 16:21; Col. 4:18; 2 Thess. 3:17–18), and sometimes just a final phrase ("Grace be with you"—2 Tim. 4:22). The letter is then rolled. A string is tied around it and clay pressed over the knot to seal it.

We today, of course, cannot know exactly the procedure Paul used or how long each letter took. We should not, though, make Paul write in our image. We should not imagine Paul locked away in a room one evening scribbling out his letter to the Corinthians. A better understanding of ancient letter writing helps us to see how truly 'weighty' Paul's letters were. He invested much time and effort in writing them. We should do the same in reading them.[53] 〞

Paul often finishes his letters with a prayer-wish. Here he wants his readers to experience peace, love with faith, and grace. All this comes from God the Father and the Lord Jesus Christ. The theme of peace runs strong through Ephesians. Paul began the letter with a greeting of peace (1:2). In 2:11–18 he stressed Jesus as our peace, the One in whom Jews and Gentiles can unite as one. In 4:1–6 we are called to keep the unity of the Spirit in the bond of peace. In 6:10–20 he speaks of the gospel of peace. God's kind of peace is deep contentment, calmness, and wholeness that come from a harmonious relationship with God. Paul wants everyone who reads this letter to experience this God-given peace.

He also wants them to know "love with faith." Paul had prayed earlier in 3:14–21 that we might know Christ's love that surpasses knowledge. He nows prays much the same thing again—that we might know in our heart of hearts how much God loves us. As we come to know God's love, we will find ourselves trusting him more and more. Paul's prayer then is

---

[53] Richards, "Paul the Letter Writer," 771.

that as we experience God's love for us at the deepest level, we will have a stronger faith and trust in him—"love with faith."

Paul closes the letter with a prayer-wish for "grace to all who love our Lord Jesus Christ with an undying love." The term "undying" translates a prepositional phrase "in incorruption" that often stands in contrast to what is mortal or corruptible (1 Cor. 15:42, 50, 53–54; 2 Tim. 1:10). The phrase could describe God's grace, which we will experience into eternity or forever. It might modify the Lord Jesus Christ, the resurrected and immortal One. Or, it could describe our love for the Lord. I like the explanation by New Testament scholar Frank Thielman, who suggests that this phrase describes our love for God as a love that is sincere and without corruption.[54]

What a way to close a letter—peace, trusting love, and grace. In a way these words sum up the whole book of Ephesians. In Christ, God has poured out his love and grace upon us. Knowing and living in his love causes us to trust him. It also leads us to honor and please the Lord in how we live, including living in peace with one another. New life in Christ leads to new community and a new walk.

So What?

1. Who are your most beloved and deeply trusted friends in the Lord? What has brought your relationship to this level?

---

[54] Thielman, *Ephesians*, 448.

2.   Sometimes when our leaders suffer, we get deeply discouraged in our faith. Paul sent Tychicus with a letter to the Ephesians to encourage them. This means Ephesians is a letter of encouragement. How has it encouraged you over the course of your study?

3.   Paul prays that the Ephesians will experience peace, love with faith, and grace. All are important, but which of these do you most need to experience at this time in life?

4.   Rather than a question, this is more an invitation. Think of someone you know who needs peace or love (with faith) or grace. Take a minute to pray this for them.

5. As you look back over your study of Ephesians, what are a couple of things the Lord has taught you that will stay with you for a long time?

I hope God has used your study of Ephesians in your life in a great way. I hope he anchored your identity in Christ. I hope you are more invested in your Christian community than ever. And I pray that you are seeing new patterns of godliness in your walk with the Lord.

All glory and honor to the Lord!

Bibliography

Arnold, Clinton E. *Ephesians*. Exegetical Commentary on the New Testament. Grand Rapids: Zondervan, 2010.

_____. *Ephesians: Power and Magic: The Concept of Power in Ephesus in Light of its Historical Situation*. SNTSMS 63. Cambridge: Cambridge University Press, 1989. Repr. Eugene, OR: Wipf & Stock, 2001.

Barna, George. *Transforming Children into Spiritual Champions: Why Children Should Be Your Church's #1 Priority*. 2d ed. Ventura, CA: Regal, 2013.

Barth, Markus. *Ephesians*. 2 vols. Anchor Bible Commentary. Garden City, NY: Doubleday, 1974.

Bruce, F. F. *The Epistles to the Colossians, to Philemon, and to the Ephesians*. New International Commentary on the New Testament. Grand Rapids: Eerdmans, 1984.

Cosgrove, Charles H. *An Ancient Christian Hymn with Musical Notation: Papyrus Oxyrhynchus 1786: Text and Commentary*. Studien und Texte zu Antike und Christentum 65. Tübingen: Mohr Siebeck, 2011.

Edwards, Mark J., ed. *Galatians, Ephesians, Philippians*. Ancient Christian Commentary on Scripture. Vol. 8. Downers Grove, IL: InterVarsity, 1999. ACCS, 8:182

Eggerichs, Emerson. *Love & Respect*. Nashville: Thomas Nelson, 2004.

Harris, Murray J. *Raised Immortal: Resurrection & Immortality in the New Testament*. Grand Rapids: Eerdmans, 1985.

Hoehner, Harold W. *Ephesians: An Exegetical Commentary*. Grand Rapids: Baker, 2002.

Hughes, R. Kent. *Ephesians: The Mystery of the Body of Christ*. Preaching the Word. Wheaton: Crossway, 1990.

Klein, William W. "Ephesians." Pages 19–193 in *The Expositor's Bible Commentary*. Rev. ed. Vol. 12. Grand Rapids: Zondervan, 2006.

_____. *The New Chosen People: A Corporate View of Election*. Eugene, OR: Wipf & Stock, 2001.

Liefeld, Walter L. *Ephesians*. The IVP New Testament Commentary. Downers Grove, IL: InterVarsity, 1997.

Lincoln, Andrew T. *Ephesians*. Word Biblical Commentary. Dallas: Word, 1990.

Lloyd-Jones, D. Martin. *God's Way of Reconciliation: An Exposition of Ephesians 2*. Grand Rapids: Baker, 1972.

Louw, Johannes P., and Eugene A. Nida. *A Greek-English Lexicon of the New Testament Based on Semantic Domains*. 2 vols. New York: United Bible Societies, 1988.

Moreland, J. P. *Love Your God with All Your Mind: The Role of Reason in the Life of the Soul*. Colorado Springs, CO: NavPress, 1997.

Morris, Leon. *Expository Reflections on the Letter to the Ephesians*. Grand Rapids: Baker, 1994.

O'Brien, Peter T. *The Letter to the Ephesians*. Pillar New Testament Commentary. Grand Rapids: Eerdmans, 1999.

Peterson, Eugene H. *Practice Resurrection: A Conversation on Growing Up in Christ*. Grand Rapids: Eerdmans, 2010.

Plantinga, Cornelius, Jr. *Not the Way It's Supposed to Be: A Breviary of Sin*. Grand Rapids: Eerdmans, 1995.

Richards, E. Randolph. "Paul the Letter Writer." In *The Baker Illustrated Bible Handbook*, ed. J. Daniel. Hays and J. Scott Duvall. Grand Rapids: Baker Books, 2011.

Smalley, Gary, and John Trent. *A Dad's Blessing*. Nashville: Thomas Nelson, 1994.

Snodgrass, Klyne. *The NIV Application Commentary: Ephesians*. Grand Rapids: Zondervan, 1996.

Stott, John R. W. *The Message of Ephesians*. Bible Speaks Today. Downers Grove, IL: InterVarsity, 1979.

Tannehill, Robert C. *Dying and Rising with Christ: A Study in Pauline Theology*. Berlin: Töppleman, 1967.

Thielman, Frank S. *Ephesians*. Baker Exegetical Commentary on the New Testament. Grand Rapids: Baker Academic, 2010.

————. "Ephesians." In *Commentary on the New Testament Use of the Old Testament*. Ed. G. K. Beale and D. A. Carson. Grand Rapids: Baker, 2007.

Trebilco, Paul. *The Early Christians in Ephesus from Paul to Ignatius*. Grand Rapids: Eerdmans, 2007.

Vaughan, W. Curtis. *The Letter to the Ephesians*. Nashville: Convention Press, 1963.

Wallace, Daniel B. *Greek Grammar Beyond the Basics: An Exegetical Syntax of the New Testament*. Grand Rapids: Zondervan, 1996.

Witherington III, Ben. *The Letters to Philemon, the Colossians, and the Ephesians: A Socio-Rhetorical Commentary on the Captivity Epistles*. Grand Rapids: Eerdmans, 2007.

Wright, Christopher J. H. "An Upside-Down World: Distinguishing between Home and Mission Field No Longer Makes Sense." *Christianity Today*. January 2007.

Wright, N. T. *The Prison Letters: Ephesians, Philippians, Colossians, and Philemon*. Paul for Everyone. Louisville: Westminster John Knox, 2004.

Printed in the United States
by Baker & Taylor Publisher Services